# Disney's Chicken Little

D1200193

# Introduction

Everyone thinks they know the story of Chicken Little—a young chicken who was hit by an acorn and thought that the sky was falling, and caused a panic when he tried to convince the other townsfolk. But is that what really happened? Disney's *Chicken Little* movie tells a bit of a different story.

Now with the games for Nintendo GameCube™, Playstation 2®, and XBOX™, as well as a portable version on the Game Boy Advance, you can play through this story yourself, putting yourself in the role of the hero and saving the day, against all odds.

This guide walks you through the console version, giving you detailed instructions on how to get past different obstacles and collect the important items. There is also a shorter guide for the GBA version, to help show you how to get to hidden places and collect the last few items you might not otherwise find.

# Characters

In each version of the Disney's CHICKEN LITTLE game, there are memorable characters for you to meet and help out—or keep from putting the hurt on Chicken Little! You'll get to know them better during the game, but here's a small introduction for you to start getting to know them better.

## Playable Characters

These are the various characters that you play in the different levels of the game. Each has his or her own personality and talents. Keep in mind that you may not be able to play every character in each version of the game.

## CHICKEN LITTLE

The hero of the story, he may be small, but he's got enough heart and guts to make up for his size. He caused a bit of a panic a while back when he claimed the sky was falling, only to be told it was an acorn. Now everyone laughs at him, but he's determined to prove himself in one way or another, and earn everyone's respect.

# FISH-OUT-OF-WATER

Behind his watery helmet he may be hard for some to understand, but Fish's friends have no problem figuring out what he has to say. Fish is cool, calm, and collected, always ready with a helping hand. Although he may be too curious for his own good!

# ABBY MALLARD

The original Ugly Duckling, Abby has clearly come to grips with her unattractive appearance. She's the grounded one in the group. As Chicken Little's best friend, she's always ready with some advice or moral support. This plucky duckling isn't about to let anything get in her way!

# TURKEY LURKEY

Turkey Lurkey is the mayor of Oakey Oaks, and while he's a bit of a pompous politician, when things get really bad he's willing to step up to the plate and defend his town himself.

# RUNT-OF-THE-LITTER

Runt is the largest of the team, and when the going gets tough, he likes to eat to calm his nerves. While most of his friends are ready for anything, Runt is a lot more easily frightened, and would much rather stay home and away from danger. When his friends are in trouble though, he's there by their side ready to help, even if he's in a panic while he does it.

# COMMANDER "ACE"

Commander Ace is a Hollywood creation. When Hollywood hears the events in Oakey Oaks, they get involved. In the movie telling, things get a bit...changed, and this is the hero of their story.

# Other Characters

While you don't actually play these characters during the game, they still have important roles in the story. As before, not every character may show up in every version.

# BUCK CLUCK

Chicken Little's father, Buck Cluck struggles to be proud of his son after the "incident," but he never stops loving him. Buck Cluck is one of Chicken Little's biggest role models, and the young chick even decides to take up baseball, a sport that his father was great at, in order to be more like him and make him proud.

# GOOSEY LOOSEY

The second half of the pair that torments the Misfits, and especially Chicken Little, Goosey is not quite as bright as her friend Foxy. Because of this, she usually ends up with the dirty jobs, keeping Foxy's hands a bit cleaner. Goosey also has a temper that Chicken Little needs to watch out for, especially with his tendency to flap off at the beak.

# FOXY LOXY

Foxy Loxy is one of the "popular crowd," a star that everyone loves—except maybe the Chicken and his friends. Behind the backs of the adults, Foxy, along with Goosey, is a bit of a bully, and her favorite target seems to be Chicken Little. She's the smart one of the pair that likes to make the friends' lives miserable.

# Multiplayer Mini-games

Over the course of each chapter you can collect sets of Buck Cluck Trading Cards. Once you pick up a few sets, trade these in to unlock different mini-games that you can then play with your friends. Each mini-game has a different goal, and different controls. They also come at different card costs, so stock up on card sets if you want to try more than one!

To purchase or play a mini-game, first load one of your game saves. Once the data is loaded, instead of choosing to "Continue Game," choose the "Extras" option. From here you can purchase mini-games from the store, play the mini-games you've already purchased, or use cheat codes for various game effects.

The various games and their costs are as follows:

| | |
|---|---|
| Drone Dash | 2 Card Sets |
| Pig Paddle | 2 Card Sets |
| Super Speedway | 5 Card Sets |
| Space Shooter | 3 Card Sets |
| Saucer Smash | 3 Card Sets |
| Walker War | 5 Card Sets |

After you're done purchasing mini-games in the store, press the button listed at the bottom of the screen to go back to the previous menu. At this point you're asked whether or not you wish to save the purchases. This lets you purchase some games to try out without saving, to see which of the games you might like best without using up your sets of cards.

## Drone Dash

**Cannon Player: Destroy the drone.**
**Drone Player: Cross the finish line.**

In this game the screen is split, with the first player's screen on top and the second player's screen on the bottom. To start with, the first player takes control of a cannon at the end of the room, while player two controls a drone. The drone must try to reach the finish line just under the cannon, while the cannon's goal is to shoot down the drone. Each time one player completes an objective, he or she earns a point.

### PS2
- Dash forward (Drone only)
- Shoot (Cannon only)
- R1 Zoom in (Cannon only)

### GC
- Dash forward (Drone only)
- Shoot (Cannon only)
- Zoom in (Cannon only)

### XBOX
- Dash forward (Drone only)
- Shoot (Cannon only)
- R Zoom in (Cannon only)

During the drone's dash forward, there are shields that it can duck behind. These are easily blasted apart by the cannon fire though, so this isn't a usable tactic for very long. The spot under the cannon's current aim is marked on the floor with a red symbol. If the player moving the drone sees this mark, he or she should get away—fast!

Round one starts with 60 seconds on the clock. Each player should try to win as many points as possible during that time. When time runs out, player one takes control of the drone while player two gets control of the cannon. Now another 60 seconds are put onto the clock. When time runs out for round two, whoever has the most points at the end is the winner.

6

# Pig Paddle

Score 10 goals (knocking Runt into the other player's side of the board) to win.

## PS2
○ Shoot

## GC
x Shoot

## XBOX
○ Shoot

For this game there is one large shared screen. The game area consists of a blue paddle for player one at the left side, a red paddle for player two to the right, and the game table itself in between. Each player is defending the opponent's goal.

Hit Runt in your goal to score a point. An added twist, you can shoot lasers from the center of your paddle, which send Runt away from you when he's struck. These shots even more than the paddle itself keep Runt away from your side, and knock him toward your challenger.

# Super Speedway

Complete 3 laps and cross the finish line before the other player.

## PS2
○ Accelerate
○ Brake
○ Reverse
L1 Powerslide
L2 Powerslide

## GC
A Accelerate
X Brake
Y Reverse
R Powerslide
L Powerslide

## XBOX
○ Accelerate
○ Brake
○ Reverse
L Powerslide
R Powerslide

This mini-game is a race, pure and simple. Player one uses the top half of the screen and the blue car, while player two uses the bottom half and the red. Each player races his or her car over the course of three full laps. Whoever reaches the finish line at the end of the third lap first wins.

The main "obstacle" for this game is the layout of the track, which may be slightly confusing. Toward the start of the race the player must take the car up a ramp, leaping across to the next part of the track.

There are also a few places where one track meets up with others joining at an intersection. At these places, remember to just take the road straight ahead. If you ever start going in the wrong direction, a "Wrong Way" indicator comes up and gives you a warning.

## Space Shooter

**Destroy enemy ships for points, and get the highest point total.**

## PS2
- Shoot
- Missile
- **L1** Tilt Left
- **R1** Tilt Right

## GC
- Fire Cannon
- Missle
- & Veer left and right. Double tap to Roll.

## XBOX
- Fire Cannon
- Missle/Fires alternative weapon
- **L** & **R** Veer left and right. Double tap to roll.

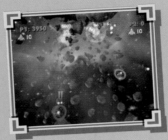

This game uses the same top-down setup as the "Space Simulator II" chapter, except now there are two "good guy" ships within the screen. The spaceship circled in blue is for player one, while the red ship is controlled by player two.

The big difference between this mini-game and the Space Simulator chapters is that the player-controlled ships do not take damage and cannot be destroyed. The goal is simply to destroy as many ships as possible, not to avoid damage. Because of this, there are no health pickups or shield pickups, although the other normal space pickups are still available after you destroy enemies or objects.

There are different enemy types for you to destroy, each of which has a different point value and behavior:

| ENEMY TYPE | POINT VALUE | BEHAVIOR |
| --- | --- | --- |
| Small, blue, round | 250 | Start in a line, slowly move around while firing, moves more directly toward bottom of screen |
| Red "robot" | 500 | Moves more quickly in a line that twists and turns at each edge of the screen, gradually winding down to the bottom |
| Orange "plane" | 750 | Moves from edge of screen toward center in a line, then "dives" for the bottom and leaves via another edge |
| Very large green ship | 1000 | Moves slowly back and forth at the top of the screen |

Occasionally another target such as an asteroid or tower will give 100 points, as well.

Both players move around the screen at the same time. The one who accumulates the most points by the time the pair reaches the finish line is the winner.

## Saucer Smash

**Destroy enemy ships for points, and the player with the most points at the end of the game wins.**

## PS2
- Shoot
- (Hold and Release) Super Shot

## GC
- (Hold and Release) Super Shot

## XBOX
- (Hold and Release) Super Shot

This game splits the screen into two, a top and bottom screen. Each player controls a cannon much like in the first section of the "Cannon Chaos" chapter, with each cannon set at an opposite corner of the town square. The idea is to swivel the cannon around and destroy the alien spaceships that appear. Each time a ship is destroyed, the player who shot it down earns a point.

Of course, a ship isn't destroyed by just one shot, so hitting a ship one time with a normal shot doesn't do anything for you. You need to use super-shots in order to win.

At the start of the game there are 60 seconds on the clock. When the time runs out, the player with the most points wins.

# Walker War

**Destroy the opponent's alien walker two times.**

## PS2

| | |
|---|---|
| **L1** | Grab/Lift |
| **L2** | Shoot/Throw |

## GC

| | |
|---|---|
| Ⓧ | Enter/Exit Walker |
| ○ | Rotate Top of Walker Control Stick Move Alien Walker |
| | Fire Cannon |
| | Pick up Object |

## XBOX

| | |
|---|---|
| | Enter and Exit Walker |
| | Rotate top of walker |
| | Move Alien Walker |
| **R** | Fire Cannon |
| **L** | Pick up Object |

Another game split into two separate screens, the Walker War pits two alien walkers against each other. The walkers can use their lasers to damage the other craft, and whoever takes the enemy out twice is the winner.

Each player's walker starts out on the opposite side of the playing field. The field itself is scattered with various objects—orange canisters, which damage anyone too close when they are shot open. The red crates which have a delayed explosion and damage anyone nearby, and the regular crates which may be thrown at an opponent but otherwise break apart harmlessly when they are picked up and thrown.

Of course, the most direct way to damage the enemy is to shoot at him or her with your laser. To help you in this, there are powerups that you can find when you break open the various objects on the field. They have a variety of effects on your laser fire, such as giving your walker the ability to shoot three lasers at once in a forked pattern, or turning your shots into more compact "bombs" of energy. Each pickup only lasts a certain amount of time, and when you pick up a new one, it replaces the old. There are also health pickups available every now and then, so keep your eyes peeled.

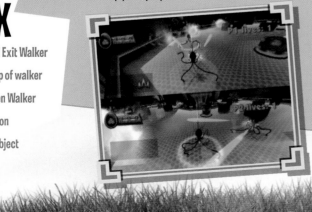

Because of the explosive objects, be careful that you don't end up damaging yourself with a careless shot or two. You also have to watch out for a crane holding an explosive canister that travels in circles around the outer edge of the playing field.

The number of lives remaining for each player is listed on his or her screen. Once a player loses both lives, the other player wins the game.

9

# Story Introduction

The events within the game CHICKEN LITTLE follow along with the events of the movie, with the bonus that you get to step into the action by directing Chicken Little through his victories and defeats. Each step of the way you must help him try to overcome Foxy Loxy, Goosey Loosey, and everyone else who would try to keep him and his friends down. Help him out, and he may yet manage to live down his one little mistake, and become somebody important after all.

## Controls

Controls within each section of the game differ to some extent, but here are some of the more common:

| Left Analog Stick / Directional Pad | Move Chicken Little around the screen. |
|---|---|
| Right Analog Stick | Move the camera to look around. |
| ✕ | The "Jump button." Most chapters use his to Jump. You may also perform a double-jump by jumping into the air, then pressing ✕ again to jump a second time before landing. |
| □ | The "Attack button." This usually allows Chicken Little to use his yoyo. It may be used to attack, to climb a pipe, or to grab onto something and swing across a gap, for starters. |
| △ | The "Grapple button." Once you pick up a special extension for the yoyo, this can be used to latch onto far-away objects and pull Chicken Little across to the target. |
| ○ | The "Aim button." Later in the game you pick up a Slingshot attachment. Press this button to aim the slingshot, and release the button to fire. Player can also tap this button to fire without aiming. |

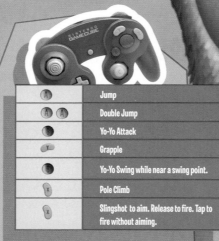

| A | Jump |
|---|---|
| A A | Double Jump |
| B | Yo-Yo Attack |
| Y | Grapple |
| B | Yo-Yo Swing while near a swing point. |
| X | Pole Climb |
| X | Slingshot to aim. Release to fire. Tap to fire without aiming. |

| | Jump |
|---|---|
| | Double Jump |
| | Yo-Yo attack |
| | Yo-Yo Grapple |
| | Yo-Yo Singwhile near a swing point. Press to Jump |
| | Pole Climb while next to a pole. |
| | Slingshot Hold to aim. Release to fire. Tap to fire without aiming. |

Each walkthrough chapter tells you the controls that you can use for that level, so don't worry too much about memorizing them all here.

# Items

Each section of the game has its own items and special locations to find. Here are some of the more important in the game and how they work.

## Acorns

These wonderful nuts increase Chicken Little's "Cluck Luck," which acts like a health meter. At the start of a chapter, Chicken Little has three eggs out of six possible in his "Cluck Luck" bar, which is located at the top left of the screen. Each time you get hit you lose one egg. If you lose all of your eggs you must start over at the last checkpoint, or at the start of the chapter if you haven't reached a checkpoint yet.

Whenever you pick up an acorn, the number to the left of Chicken Little's Cluck Luck meter goes up by one. Whenever you collect enough acorns in a level you regain one egg. You can never go over the maximum number of eggs. However, on Easy Mode you need five acorns to regenerate an egg, while on Normal Mode you need 10, and for Hard Mode you have to collect 15.

## Buck Cluck Trading Cards

Some chapters have cards scattered throughout its levels. Complete a set by collecting all five cards before moving on. They don't carry over from one chapter to the next, so make sure you have them before moving on. Check the number of cards you've found in the level at the bottom left of the screen. Not every chapter has cards for you to collect, but most do.

Once you have a few sets of trading cards, stop by the Minigame Store in the Game Menu. Here you can trade in sets of cards to unlock various minigames to play with your friends.

## Checkpoints

To activate a checkpoint, simply have Chicken Little touch it. Be careful—hitting a Checkpoint does not save your game to the memory card. If you turn your console off without actually saving, you'll have to start over again when you turn the game back on.

## Point of Interest

This marks some spot that's important to the game. Approaching the "?" with your character tells you what you need to do, or lets you take an important action if you've completed your task.

# Game Difficulty

Whenever you start a new game you also have to choose the game's difficulty level. This has two main effects.

First, as mentioned above, the difficulty determines how many acorns you need to collect to earn each egg. For easy mode you only need 5 acorns, for Normal you need 10, and for Hard Mode you have to pick up 15 acorns per egg.

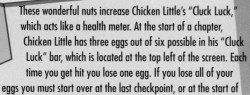

Also, for the chapters where you must collect coins to finish a task, the game difficulty determines how many you need. In Easy mode you need 10 coins, in Normal you need 15, and in Hard Mode you need to pick up all 20 coins within a level to finish the job.

# Using the Walkthrough

Whenever you start a new game you also have to choose the game's difficulty level. This has two main effects.

First, as mentioned above, the difficulty determines how many acorns you need to collect to earn each egg. For easy mode you only need 5 acorns, for Normal you need 10, and for Hard Mode you have to pick up 15 acorns per egg.

Also, for the chapters where you must collect coins to finish a task, the game difficulty determines how many you need. In Easy mode you need 10 coins, in Normal you need 15, and in Hard Mode you need to pick up all 20 coins within a level to finish the job.

## Controls

This is a list of the detailed controls for the level. This is especially important for the chapters where you don't play as Chicken Little—for example, the Space Simulator levels where you guide a spaceship, or the chapters where you guide Fish or Runt through different tubes and slides.

## Items

These are items of note that you pick up or actually use over the course of the level. For instance, if you need to collect coins to buy a soda, or pick up a bundle of items to run an errand, you find the item listed here. Keep an eye out for them!

## Dangers

This is a list of things you have to watch out for. They take away an egg (or health from a mechanical object like a spaceship or alien walker). If you see something listed here, keep a close eye out for it throughout the chapter to avoid a possible setback!

# Late for School

Thanks to being unpopular after his...incident, and being left behind by the morning bus, Chicken Little is running late for school. Again. But with a little creativity in his route, he still might be able to make it before roll is called. Guide Chicken Little to school, and get him into class on time!

## PS2

Jump
Double Jump
Yo-yo Attack
Pole Climb

## GC

Jump
Double Jump
Yo-yo Attack
Pole Climb

## XBOX

Jump
Double Jump
Yo-yo Attack
Pole Climb

## ITEMS

Coins
There are 20 scattered around the schoolyard. Collect 15 to buy a soda from the machine.

## DANGERS

Don't fall from too high!

Watch out for hot steam—wait for it to stop before you pass.

Avoid barricades while sliding down a pipe by jumping.

Don't let the Chicken Little toys explode nearby!

Be careful not to hit anything when rocketing through the air.

## Get to School!

Chicken Little starts out on a hilltop high above the school, looking for the best way to get down. Run across the wooden bridge and gather the acorns to start building toward his next egg, displayed at the upper left of the screen. Follow the ledge around and double-jump between the rocks, and over to the next high point. At the end of this cliff you find your first checkpoint, and just behind it are garbage bags and barricades—attack them, breaking them open to collect more acorns.

Once the clutter is out of the way press forward to run along the pipe to the next cliff. Don't fall, and watch out for the steam coming out of the pipe—wait until it dies down to run past it. At the end of the pipe is another checkpoint. Pass it, and double jump up to the lowest rock, and leap to the next rock and then the next highest ledge where you find your first **card**.

When you pick up the card turn around and run along the ledge, breaking up some barricades to get past. Jump over the gaps to the next two bits of ledge, then jump up along the stone "steps" to higher ground. At the top of the hill break the barricades to find a pipe sticking up.

At the end of this cliff fight off the toy and then destroy the barricade. Here is another pipe to run along, with more steam to watch out for. At the end of the pipe destroy the next barriers, and fight the next three toys. One is just ahead, and another is on each of the next ledges you jump to.

Run up to the pipe and wrap your yo-yo around the pipe. Press up on the analog stick or directional pad to climb the pipe. Once you reach the top you slide along a cable to a wooden platform beside a water tower, and another checkpoint.

On top of the highest ledge, there are two sets of barricades. Attack the one to the left to find a second **card**. Now destroy the other barricades to reveal another pipe to climb. At the top you have one more set of cables to slide down, and when you reach the bottom you find another checkpoint, and the school.

Now you jump from one wooden platform to another, in a circle around the water tower. Be careful not to slip, because it's a long way down! At the end of the circle you find another pipe. Climb it, and when you get to the top you slide from the pipe to the top of the water tower. Collect the acorns and hit the checkpoint, then search to find another kind of pipe attached to the edge of the roof.

Step onto this other pipe to start a long slide down. When you slide toward a barricade jump over it, or else you'll lose an egg when you hit it. There are also some acorns at places just high enough over the pipe that you have to jump if you want to collect them.

# School's In Session

Chicken Little's made it to school, but now he finds the door already shut and locked. He looks around for a way to get in, and spots a soda machine, which gives him an idea. To get a bottle of soda you need to collect coins. The number changes with the difficulty settings. Once you collect enough, run up to the "?" marking a point of interest in front of the soda machine.

## On the Playground

When you face the school, the playground is to your right. On the playground you find a red, yellow and blue jungle gym that leads to a lot of the places you want to go. But watch out for the box of Chicken Little toys nearby! It keeps spitting out toys constantly, and there's no way to stop it.

## Mad Merchandise

At the end of the pipe a new danger appears. Some of the Chicken Little toy figures being sold around town are running loose. They start to talk faster and faster, and then explode. If you're too close when they blow up, you lose one of your eggs. Run up to them when you see them and attack with your yo-yo, but be careful they don't jump out of the way! If you manage to destroy one it drops two acorns, but these acorns vanish after a short time.

13

Avoid or fight any of the toys that come out of the box, and jump up onto one of the lower platforms of the jungle gym. In one of the blue tubes inside it you find one of the coins. Now jump up around the platforms on the outside of the jungle gym to reach a blue "room." From here you can step out onto a pipe running all around the jungle gym. Run all along this to find a few acorns, and another of the coins you need.

From the edge of the platform closest to the pipe, run around the corner of the building and onto the top of a furnace, being careful not to run into the steam when it jets out. When it's safe, run past onto another wooden platform with a can of paint, then turn the corner to destroy two more cans. Past the last two paint cans is another jet of steam, and finally another coin.

When you're done run back to the blue "room," and run out another exit to find a pole leading up. Climb the pole, and slide down the cable to a yellow roof on the jungle gym. Here you find another pole leading up that you should climb. Once you reach the top you slide down onto a water tank, with a coin on top of it. You also find a checkpoint here. Now you're in the pipe-slide section of the schoolyard.

From the last corner look carefully to find a set of stumps in the nearby woods that you can double-jump to, double-jumping between them to reach the tallest stump and a **card** on top of it. From here jump down to land inside the woods.

## In the Woods

This small wooded area holds a few other interesting pieces. Toward the front of the school you find more stumps—this time you can reach the shortest one by double-jumping from the ground, then leap between stumps and boulders higher and higher to finally reach a coin.

Just be careful when exploring this area, since sometimes the Chicken Little toys may wander over from the playground, and you might have to fight one or two. When you pick up everything else, run back over to the playground, and climb the jungle gym again back to the top of the yellow roof.

## The Pipe-Slide

From the top of the water tank, step onto the pipe at one end to start your slide. Partway down the pipe you start to see more barricades that you have to jump over. On the bright side, there are also three coins along the pipe itself that you pick up along the way. When you reach the end of the pipe you slide onto a wooden platform. Pick up another coin on this platform, and attack the paint cans here to destroy them and pick up some more acorns.

You can also jump down at the end of the first section of cable to land on a hilltop, gather the coins and acorns, then climb the pole to continue on to the front of the school! Either way is fine—it doesn't matter what order you collect the coins in, as long as you collect enough.

This time instead of climbing the pole on top of the yellow roof, double-jump over to a red section of roof to reach a second pole. From the top you slide down another cable, which leads to a few interesting places.

Drop to the ground below while sliding down the cable. If you time this right, you can land on top of the bus to collect a **card**. Now jump down, run back to the playground, and climb back up to the red roof to take the same cable slide again.

## Climbing the Walls

At the end of the set of cables you end up on a ledge along the front of the school itself. Destroy the flower pots to collect acorns, then climb up the pipe at the end of the ledge. From higher up on the pipe jump down to a higher ledge, and follow it to above the school's doorway. Here you find two more coins to collect.

When you're done, run back to the ledge you first landed on from the cables. If you jump carefully you can reach another set of stumps, this time on the other side of the school. The top stump here holds another coin. If you miss your jump, you can get onto the shortest stump in the chain from the ground level. Also on the ground you find a set of bags in a corner beside the school, which you can destroy to grab a couple acorns.

When you're done here, explore this same section of lawn carefully. In between some of the trees you find a coin tucked away, and nearby you can climb a slope onto the top of a small hill. On the hill you find a group of Chicken Little toys, but also two more coins. If you haven't missed any, this should give you enough for a soda. If you have missed some and don't want to go back for them, keep going to collect some of the last five. You can either jump back down to the lawn from here, or climb up the pole to slide back to the ledges on the front of the school.

15

## Paved Over

Now from the lawn, run back toward the front of the school and follow the paved road. There is another box of Chicken Little toys beside the school bus, but you want to pass it by and run down toward the gate in front of the school, where you find a coin and a few acorns.

Step up to the "?" in front of the machine, and when the box comes up choose "yes" to buy a bottle of pop. When it comes out, Chicken Little straps the soda bottle onto his back and uses it to launch into the air, ready to enter the school through an unusual entrance.

If you're running low on eggs and are good at fighting the Chicken Little toys; hang around the side of the bus for a while and destroy the toys as they appear; which lets you collect a lot of acorns to restore some of your missing eggs.

Now run back up the pavement and enter the playground again. Finally head past the jungle gym, veer toward the soda machine, and run past it to the corner of the fence. Jump on top of the boxes to reach a coin and another pole. Climb the pole and slide along the cable to reach the roof of the school. Here are two more coins, and one last pole.

Climb the pole, and this time you slide down a cable onto a set of fungus growing off the side of a tree. The last coin is here. Grab it and jump down, then run back through the playground to the soda machine.

## Bottle Rocket

During this flight, the only controls you can use are the analog stick or directional pad, to steer your flight. The risk here lies in crashing into anything—with the soda on his back, Chicken Little is moving so fast that hitting anything is dangerous.

Steer over the first white fence, and around the trees that come after it. Now you start to fly through tunnels in the nearby rock. In the first tunnel you should steer right, then left. In the next short tunnel fly up, down, right, and up again.

Now you're back in the open, which means it's time to dodge a few more trees before the next section of tunnel. When you reach it, this time go left, up, and right. In the last tunnel fly down under the barrier, then be ready. As you fly out of the tunnel aim for between the poles holding up the pipe-slide, to grab the last **card**. Dodge around the next poles and a few last trees before flying in through an open window, and into the school at last. Make sure you save your game before going on to the next section.

16

# Dodgeball Hall

Although he's made it into the school, Chicken Little still has to make a mad dash for class. Get him through the halls to gym class, and then help his dodgeball team stomp the other team into the ground.

## PS2

**Dodgeball Hall:**
- ⊗ Jump

**Dodgeball Game:**
- Move
- Dodge and Throw

## GC

**Dodgeball Hall:**
- Ⓐ Jump

**Dodgeball Game:**
- Move
- Ⓐ Dodge and Throw

## XBOX

**Dodgeball Hall:**
- Jump

**Dodgeball Game:**
- Ⓛ Move
- Dodge and Throw

## ITEMS

**Dodgeball**

Pick up a ball during the dodgeball game to throw it back at the other team and knock a player out of the match!

## DANGERS

Jump over or move around the lockers, carts, and other objects that fall into your path.

Avoid running into the pillars in the middle of the halls.

Don't get hit by a ball during the dodgeball game.

## Dodgeball Hall

In his scramble to get to class after coming in through the window, Chicken Little steps into a janitor's soapy pail and starts flying through the halls faster than he'd intended. Now you have to keep him from smashing into anything on the way to the gym. Other than moving him from side to side with the left analog stick or directional pad, the only control you can use is a normal jump.

The first section of hallway holds no real danger, but there are a few acorns to collect. The acorns are important because each time you crash into something, you lose an egg and have to start all over again, or at least go back at the last checkpoint you crossed (which is marked by a chiming tone).

After Chicken Little crashes through the first set of doors in his bucket, a locker falls into his path. Make your jump as prompted, just before you reach the lockers, and you soar over the obstacle to safety... until a set of lockers crashes down from the left before the next set of double doors.

17

Each time a set of lockers falls into your path, you have to jump over them, or move around them to the side if there's any space there. Stacks of books are okay—you can crash through them without any trouble. Through the next set of doors is a pillar in the center of the hall. You have to move around this, since you can't jump over it. If you go past it on the right, there's a locker on the ground that you have to jump. Swing back behind the pillar quickly to pick up a **card** on your way past.

In the next section of hallway, you have a locker falling to the left, a pillar, and then a locker that falls only partway over to the right. In the section after that, a teacher pushes a cart into the hallway from the right, which you must avoid. Go just around it to the left, and jump again to reach the second **card**. Then be ready for another jump over a pair of lockers. You have to make a well-timed leap to clear them both.

Through the next doors are three pillars, the first to the left and the second to the right, with the third to the left again. Go past the first pillar just to the right, and the second to the left. Then swing right again. As you get close to the third pillar, a locker falls from the left, blocking that side more completely.

Just past the next door, a locker falls partway along the left side without warning, so hit the doors more toward the right of the hall. Most of the rest of the section is clear, with just a fallen locker partially blocking the left side of the hall at the end. In the next section, a locker falls from the right, followed by a cabinet from the left. The cabinet is wide and harder to clear with a jump, but if you manage it, you can pick up a third card hanging in the air just above it.

The next section has lockers falling from the right and left, and a cabinet from the right. Past the next set of doors, a locker drops from the right, another drops from the left, and another one falls on top of it from the right. This means you have to jump over the lower locker on the left side, followed by another jump to clear one last locker that falls from the left before the double doors.

Now another pair of lockers fall, giving you a wide jump to clear. Move toward the right to pick up the **card** that's revealed as a door closes, jumping as you grab it to clear the locker that falls from the right. In the next section of hallway, another pair of lockers fall. You have to jump to the left side to avoid the higher locker, with a wide cabinet coming from the left farther down the hall. After the cabinet, a locker falls again from the left, but you should swerve to the right and jump to collect the last **card** just before the mad dash comes to an end at the gym.

# Dodgeball Game

When Chicken Little reaches the gym, he can't stop to catch his breath just yet. Today's physical education class includes a game of dodgeball, with the unpopular kids vs. the popular kids. You control Chicken Little throughout the game, and you need to win a total of three games to move on to the next chapter.

Aside from moving around as usual, the only other button to press is the dodge button. This button makes you dash quickly to dodge out of the way, and if you're holding a ball, this button throws it. Chicken Little is marked with a green circle and an arrow showing the direction he's facing, so you shouldn't lose track of him even with so many people and projectiles flying around.

To win a game, your team needs to take out all of Foxy's team members by hitting them one by one with a dodgeball. Your team members will also aim for the other team, with a red circle marking anyone else holding a ball, but whenever someone from either side takes a hit they're out of the game. Chicken Little has three eggs to start each game of dodgeball. Each time he gets hit he loses an egg, so he can be hit three times before sitting out. Once Chicken Little is out, your team loses.

When a game starts, both sides run for the line of balls in the center of the court and then start throwing. Since everyone is dashing up to the front, it's a good idea to hang back and be ready to dodge. Once the other team throws a ball at you and misses, you can run over to pick it up.

When you have a ball, run up toward the line and make sure you have a good shot at one of the other team. Aim carefully with the left analog stick or directional buttons. Then throw the ball and try to take out one of Foxy's team. Just make sure that the other team isn't about to take *you* out. If they're coming close, throw the ball and be ready to dodge. If you're down to just Chicken Little, you might want to wait for the other team to throw all of the balls to your side. Then you can pick one up and aim more carefully, without worrying about being hit.

If you win three games before the other team does, the chapter comes to an end. Chicken Little's team loses if Chicken Little is out.

# Goosey Chase

Once again, running off at the mouth without thinking has gotten Chicken Little into trouble. He's made Goosey Loosey as mad as a wet hen, and if she catches him, Chicken Little's goose is cooked! It's time for another wild goose chase through the halls of the school, while you keep Chicken Little safe from Goosey.

## PS2
- Jump
- Double Jump
- Yo-yo Attack

## GC
- Jump
- Double Jump
- Yo-yo Attack

## XBOX
- Jump
- Double Jump
- Yo-yo Attack

## DANGERS

Getting hit with a dodgeball takes away one egg.

Don't let Goosey catch Chicken Little, or he's had it!

19

# Wild Goose Chase

On this trip through the hallways, you're coming the opposite way, and there's no handy bucket to help you move quickly. This time you have to use the left analog stick or directional pad to keep running toward the camera, and at the same time jump over, run around, or destroy the objects in your path. You must keep moving as quickly as possible, or else Goosey is going to catch Chicken Little and turn him into chicken soup!

If Goosey lunges and catches Chicken Little, you have to start the chase all over again. If she throws a dodgeball and hits Chicken Little, he loses an egg. This also knocks him off his feet and slows him down a bit. Watch for Goosey's hands to start glowing, and then be ready to quickly dodge to one side as she throws the ball.

In the first hallway, follow the line of acorns and jump over the three lockers in your path. Then, either run around the garbage can or smash it with your yo-yo. Run past the lockers through the next doors toward the left side of the screen. Then run quickly to the right to avoid the pool of water. These puddles cause Chicken Little to slip and slide, slowing him down. Another group of lockers is to the right after the puddle. Run up the locker sitting at an angle, jump off the end, and pick up your first **card** for the chapter.

In the next section, you have a garbage can and two lockers to navigate, and then another set of lockers with the first leaning up at an angle. This time the upper locker holds only an acorn at the end. Make your way past two more lockers on the ground, and another trash can.

Through the next doors, you have a bit of a break. There's a pool of water to the left, but there's also a wheeled dolly. If you jump onto the dolly, it whisks you down the hall at high speed, helping you get farther away from Goosey. The catch is that this causes you to miss a **card** along the right side of the hall. The first time through, you should go to the right of the dolly and run down the hall under your own power, grabbing the card on the way.

The next section of hallway is trickier. There's water to the left and to the right, with lockers to jump in the middle. Stick mostly to the middle at first. After the pool of water to the right, the rest of the water is along the left wall. Move to the other side and run around some of the lockers that way. Stay to the right as you go through the doors, and jump along a pair of lockers to reach the next **card**. Watch out for water along the left and a wide set of lockers after it to the right. Move toward the left side of the hall to avoid a higher locker that you can't jump or climb over, and dash for the next doors.

When you see the wide set of lockers to the left, jump on them, and jump off the other end to reach the fourth **card**. Watch out for a teacher coming out of a room with a cart, and a locker to the right after that. Next is a trash can in the center of the hall, a set of lockers with a high one to the right blocking your path, followed quickly by a puddle of water to the left.

When you get to the next set of doors, you're on the home stretch. A pair of lockers blocks the hall just after the doors, forcing you to climb over. Stay to the right side to grab the last **card** on your way over, unfortunately in the center of a pool of water. You have a locker, a trash can, another locker, and another trash can in this stretch of hallway, and then a locker along the left of the next section.

As the bell rings, students rush out from every door! Do your best to push through them and avoid a locker to the right, followed by one more to the left. And then safety! (Or is it…?)

# Uniform Hunt

After such a hard chase, Chicken Little should be safe, but things don't always work out as they should. Although he survived the encounter, he still got himself into trouble with the principal, while Goosey got off free as a bird. To redeem himself, he decides to follow in his father's high-school footsteps and take up baseball. With Chicken Little's first game approaching, Foxy Loxy decides to cause him even more problems and hide pieces of his uniform all over town! Help Chicken Little find the parts of his uniform and make it to the game on time.

Walkthrough

## PS2

- Jump
- Double Jump
- Yo-yo Attack
- Pole Climb
- Jump, Attack
- Grapple (After grapple upgrade)

## GC

- Jump
- Double Jump
- Yo-yo Attack
- Pole Climb
- Jump, Attack
- Grapple (After grapple upgrade)

## XBOX

- Jump
- Double Jump
- Yo-yo Attack
- Pole Climb
- Jump, Attack
- Grapple (After grapple upgrade)

## ITEMS

**Helmet**
Collect this piece of your uniform.

**Jersey**
Collect this piece of your uniform.

**Bat**
Collect this piece of your uniform.

**Mitt**
Collect this piece of your uniform.

**Pants**
Collect this piece of your uniform.

**Cleats**
Collect this piece of your uniform.

**Grapple Upgrade**
Grab this item so Chicken Little can grapple objects and pull himself forward.

## DANGERS

Avoid the Chicken Little toys when they're near you or explode into pieces.

Don't fall down the open manhole!

Beware of steam coming from the pipes.

Inside the theater, avoid the worn-out cushions.

Falling from the highest levels inside the theater hurts, so watch your step!

# Alley·Cat

At the start of the hunt, Chicken Little is at the end of an alley, with a few fences in the way. You need a bit of creativity to get past them and find the pieces of his uniform.

Turn Chicken Little toward his left, and run into the narrow place between the fence and building. Don't forget to break open the garbage bags and cans of paint to collect more acorns. When you reach the corner of the fence, turn to the right to collect the first **card** in this area. Be ready to fight off the Chicken Little toys that are jumping around nearby.

Run toward the center of this fenced-in section, and attack a stack of three boxes propping up a board. When one end of the board falls to the ground, run up the slope to reach the top of a dumpster. Jump up onto the ledge to grab a grappling upgrade for your yo-yo. This lets you grapple a far-off object and pull yourself across gaps.

You get your chance to try out this upgrade now. Turn toward the end of the ledge. When the prompt appears, shoot out your yo-yo and grab a far-off hook. This pulls you forward to land on another ledge. Climb up the pipe to the side of the ledge, and slide along the wire to reach another roof. Run along the plank and double jump to a white platform. Then use the grapple again to reach a wooden walkway.

Run along the walkway, and then jump off the end to a white board jutting out. Turn and run along this board to leap to a series of wooden platforms, each holding an acorn. The first platform gives you access to another pipe to climb, but be quick. If you stand on the wooden platforms too long, they fall to the ground, dropping Chicken Little behind the first section of fence.

Grab onto the pipe quickly, and climb up to another set of platforms to pick up the second **card**. Then jump back down to the first set of platforms. If you fall, there's a pipe leading back up to the white wooden walkway beside one of the fences. Just be careful of Chicken Little toys while you're on the ground, and don't step into the open manhole. This takes away one of your eggs.

If you jump straight ahead along the lower wooden platforms, you reach a longer, more stable platform. This leads to a section of pipe to run along, with more jets of steam to avoid. At the end of this pipe is another pipe leading straight up. Climb it to reach a white platform. From there, step onto a pipe-slide leading to another roof.

## Swingin' Good Time

At the edge of this roof, you have another trick to learn. Face the pole sticking out of the wall, jump toward it, grab the pole with your yo-yo. Swing back and forth a few times to get used to the rhythm. Then, when you're at the farthest part of your swing, jump onto a white platform. If you fall, another pipe nearby takes you back up to the previous roof.

Now jump from platform to platform until you get to a white wooden board jutting out a bit over the road. Use your grapple upgrade to grab onto a hook across the street. Then use the jump and yo-yo-grab combination to swing across the next fence onto a ledge.

Now return to the roof, climb the pipe, and slide along the cable to land on another roof across the street. There are two Chicken Little toys to destroy this time, and one last pipe. This time when you climb the pipe, you reach your **helmet**—the first piece of your uniform! Continue to climb after you pick up the helmet, and you slide down a series of cables to reach the town square.

Walkthrough

Watch out for steam coming from pipes as you run along the ledge collecting acorns. When you reach the pipe, climb up to the cable and slide down to another white wooden ledge back across the street. Double jump over to a gray roof. Here you find a group of pipes leading up and a short narrow ledge with a few acorns nearby. Latch onto the right-hand pipe and climb up. At the top, jump over toward the second pipe and quickly latch on with your yo-yo. Do the same with the next pipe, and from there, jump onto a white wooden platform. Run off the edge to jump between more of the rickety wooden platforms, and then onto another pipe leading up.

# Hip·to·Be·Square

When you land in the town square, there are more pieces of the uniform to collect. The first is easy to claim. Run up to the tree in the center of the square. You find some fungi on the trunk, which you can use like steps. From the top fungus, jump over to a white board. Before the board has a chance to tilt very far, run to the other edge and jump over to another group of boards, where you find your uniform **jersey**.

At the top of this pipe, jump onto the roof and fight off the Chicken Little toy guarding it. Then follow the wooden plank down to the next roof. There's another Chicken Little toy here, as well as a pipe leading back up to the cable. There's also a ledge straight ahead from where you came down onto the roof. Climb onto it and carefully pick up the third **card.**

Jump back down to the ground. Run along the inside edge of the buildings in the square until you find a group of crates next to the fire station. It looks like a bull's-eye is stretched over top of them. Jump up onto the ledge next to the crates, and then leap onto the bull's-eye. This acts as a trampoline. Use it to jump onto the blue roof, where you find your **bat**.

23

Now jump off the other edge of the roof, and keep running along the fronts of the buildings until you reach a pipe that you can climb. From the pipe, jump onto the brown awning and collect your **mitt**. This leaves just two more pieces of uniform to go.

Inside the square, find a building with open doors and an arrow pointing inside. This is the movie theater. Run inside to find your last two uniform pieces.

Near your catcher's mitt is a street leading to the front of the ballpark. Don't bother running over there until you collect your full uniform. Without it, Foxy will just mock Chicken Little and turn him away.

# Late for the Movie

When you reach the lobby of the theater, run through the right-hand door and go down one of the aisles. Along the way, you see buckets of popcorn. Break them open and collect more acorns.

Now that you've found most of your uniform, it's time to concentrate on the final two cards. Return to the fire station, near where you found your bat, and climb up a lamppost on a nearby corner. At the top, slide down a cable onto a flat bit of black rooftop. Follow this narrow path and jump onto a slanting brown roof, on top of which you find one of the missing **cards**.

Now jump onto one of the open seats in the front row of the theater. The cushion acts like a trampoline and sends you high into the air. Face the back of the theater, then jump toward one of the other open, dark-blue seats. Avoid the lighter-blue seats with springs showing through. These will snap shut on Chicken Little and hurt him, taking away one egg and making you start back at the last checkpoint.

Jump back down to the ground and continue in the same general direction, away from the firehouse to the front of the town hall. At the far corner inside the square, you can jump to the base of another pole from a nearby bench. Climb this pole to pick up the last **card** near the top.

Jump along the open seats until you reach the fourth row. When you reach the top of your next jump, move over to the balcony. Jump onto the open chairs in the front balcony row. Turn to face the right, if you were facing the back before. Double jump forward when you reach the top of your jump from the chair, and use your yo-yo. If you time it right, you should latch onto a wire running from the back of the theater toward the front.

When you grab the wire with your yo-yo, you slide down to a platform above the big screen. Be careful not to go too far and fall off, or you have to climb all the way back to the top again. From the platform, jump onto a walkway that runs over top of the screen. Then keep going straight along the walkway leading behind the curtains. If you fall once you're behind the scenes, you have to fight off a group of Chicken Little toys. Then climb back up to the higher level using a pipe at one end of the room.

When it's safe, jump up from one platform to the next, and climb onto a metal walkway. Climb up another pipe at the end. Halfway up, you find your uniform's **pants**. Continue up the pipe to reach a higher walkway, where you must fight a Chicken Little toy on your way to the next edge. Be careful not to fall from the higher levels of the theater, or else you have to climb all the way back up.

When you reach the end of the platform, turn toward the center of the room, and jump from the edge closest to a pole jutting out. Grab onto it with your yo-yo and swing over to the next wooden platform. At the far end, turn to the right and break another sandbag. This causes a metal walkway to lower so that you can run up onto it.

## Behind the Scenes

At the end of the walkway, jump onto a board hanging by a rope. Don't stand still once you land on this board, or it will tilt over too far and dump you onto the ground. Go to the other end, and jump to the next platform. At one end, destroy the sandbag hanging down, which causes a pipe to fall slightly until it connects with your current platform.

At the end of the walkway, jump over to another of the tilting boards. Run along it and quickly jump over to the next section. Run along these final walkways to the top of the theater, and you find your missing **cleats**. Pick them up and walk out the exit marked with a red arrow.

Run along the pipe to reach a new platform, and then turn and run out along a board to the platform's side. From the end of the board, double jump to a white platform hanging on its own. Then continue from there to a metal platform. Turn and run along the top of the screen onto some metal stairs. From the top of these stairs, watch the nearby white platforms. There are three platforms that move around slowly, and you must time your jump to each one when it's as close to you as possible.

When you're out on the rooftop of the theater, climb the pole and slide down the cables to the town square. Run to the front of the baseball field nearby. Foxy is gone, and in her place is a red arrow marking the exit. Go through the exit to save, as Chicken Little makes it to the game on time.

25

# Batting Practice

With his uniform on, Chicken Little is almost ready to go! Before he plays in the big game, though, he needs to get in a bit of batting practice to make sure he has the skills to wow the crowd. Help Chicken Little bat in three runs to warm up for the main attraction.

## PS2
- ✕ Press when ✕ crosses plate.
- ○ Press when ○ crosses plate.
- □ Press when □ crosses plate.
- △ Press when △ crosses plate.

## GC
- Ⓐ Press when Ⓐ crosses plate.
- Ⓑ Press when Ⓑ crosses plate.
- Ⓨ Press when Ⓨ crosses plate.
- Ⓧ Press when Ⓧ crosses plate.

## XBOX
- Ⓐ Press when Ⓐ crosses plate.
- Ⓧ Press when Ⓧ crosses plate.
- Ⓨ Press when Ⓨ crosses plate.
- Ⓑ Press when Ⓑ crosses plate.

## Batter Up!

In batting practice, the controls and displays are different from what you're used to. In the bottom-right corner of the screen is a miniature baseball diamond, showing where any runners are standing and any runs you've batted in so far. To finish this batting practice, you don't need to actually hit a home run—you just need to get three runners around the bases.

When Chicken Little is at the plate and you're ready to swing the bat, start practice. Listen to the music and watch the symbols move across the top of the screen. The button symbols move left across the bar, and you need to press the correct button just as the symbol crosses the home plate. The more symbols you get right, the better chance you have for a good hit when you swing at the ball.

At the start of batting practice, four symbols in a row are all the same button, giving you a bit of an easy start. As you practice, the buttons change more often and you have to enter more of them. Be on your toes.

If you miss three of the symbols in a row and get three X's at the top of the bar, Chicken Little misses the ball entirely. If you get enough of them right, though, Abby pitches the ball and it's up to you to make sure the bat connects. This time a ball floats across the top of the screen, and you need to press the button when it's inside the red, yellow and orange bar over home plate.

The closer the ball is to the center of the red, yellow and orange bar when you press the button, the better your hit. If you just catch the edge of the ball in the zone, you hit a single. The more symbols you got right during the song, and the closer to home plate they were when you hit the buttons, the larger the zone around home plate is.

Watch the diamond in the bottom-right corner of the screen to see how well you're doing. A baseball cap appears where a runner would be on base, if this were an actual game. Below the diamond, you see the number of runs out of three that you have so far.

Once you have enough runs, you can save your game and continue to the Big Game itself, or you can get in a few more practice pitches if you're not feeling confident yet. Don't worry about striking out a few times. This is just practice and there are no eggs to be lost, so missing the ball a few times just means practice takes a bit longer.

# The Big Game

Now that Chicken Little has some batting practice under his belt, it's his turn to step up to bat for real. His new team, the Acorns, hasn't won the pennant in a very long time. If he can help them win this game, it'll male the townspeople forget about his mistakes in the past. Make sure Chicken Little's dream comes true by getting him that winning hit!

Walkthrough

## PS2
- ✕ Press when ✕ crosses plate.
- ⊙ Press when ⊙ crosses plate.
- ☐ Press when ☐ crosses plate.
- △ Press when △ crosses plate.

## GC
- Ⓐ Press when Ⓐ crosses plate.
- Ⓑ Press when Ⓑ crosses plate.
- Ⓨ Press when Ⓨ crosses plate.
- Ⓧ Press when Ⓧ crosses plate.

## XBOX
- Ⓧ Press when Ⓧ crosses plate.
- Ⓐ Press when Ⓐ crosses plate.
- Ⓨ Press when Ⓨ crosses plate.
- Ⓑ Press when Ⓑ crosses plate.

## Peanuts and Popcorn

The setup is the same as in batting practice, except this time you don't need to get in a number of runs. You just need to connect with the ball to get the winning hit in front of the adoring crowd.

The mechanics are the same as in batting practice. Push the correct buttons as the symbols move across the top of the screen into the home plate zone. The more symbols you get right, the better your zone for hitting the ball.

All you need do is connect with the ball one time without hitting a foul (which happens when you connect while the ball is in one of the outer zones). Don't worry if you miss or foul. You just get to try again. Once you connect with the ball, Chicken Little's team is victorious, and he comes out of the game a hero instead of a zero!

# Carpool Craze

After the big game, all is well in Chicken Little's world. He's a big hero, his "incident" seems to have been forgotten, his father is proud and the sky is falling... *The sky is falling?!?*

When Chicken Little calls for help in finding out what's going on, his misfit friends are on the case—after they run a few errands. Direct their car around town to finish up their various chores, and help them get to Chicken Little's side as fast as they can.

## PS2
- ✕ Accelerate
- ⊙ Brake
- △ Reverse
- ☐ Throw an object (on the paper route or a food delivery errand)
- **L1** Powerslide
- **R1** Powerslide

## GC
- Ⓒ Steer
- Ⓐ Accelerate
- Ⓨ Reverse
- Ⓧ Brake
- Ⓡ or Ⓛ Power Slide

## XBOX
- Ⓛ Steer
- Ⓐ Accelerate
- Ⓨ Reverse
- Ⓑ Brake
- Ⓡ Powerslide

## DANGERS

Don't let your clock run out on the errands with a time limit.

27

# ITEMS

| | |
|---|---|
| **Clock**  | Add five seconds to your time (on timed errands). |
| **Snacks**  | Pick up three within 50 seconds. |
| **Surfboards**  | Pick up the bundle of surfboards, then deliver the surfboards to four separate houses. |
| **Magazine**  | Collect three of these for an errand. |

| | |
|---|---|
| **Newspaper Bundle** | Drive through the bundle to pick it up, and then throw the newspapers at the houses on the route. |
| **Trough** | Pick up this container to start collecting groceries, and deliver it again when you're done. |
| **Groceries** | Four of these fill up the trough. |
| **Cookies**  | This lets you throw the food to five locations that require delivery. |

## Don't-Try-This at Home!

### Since some of the errands involve moving around town to fetch items under a certain time limit, it's a good idea to drive around a bit now to get a better idea of the layout of the town.

Chicken's friends are a bit crazy behind the wheel, but that won't keep them from their tasks. Luckily in this scenario, hitting another car or object won't do any permanent damage, but it does slow down the group during their timed errands. On each errand, you drive to one or more places, marked on the mini-map in the top-right corner of the screen. They're also marked by a beacon seen from afar on the main screen, as well as by arrows.

Your first goal is to pull up in front of Abby's house to take care of something she's forgotten, so follow the arrow and beacon to her house. You can drive cross-country in some places if you don't want to follow the roads, but beware of large fences and houses. You can't drive through these, although some smaller fences and other flimsy objects will be crushed as you drive through them.

Once you reach Abby's house, drive up to touch the exclamation point ("!") in her driveway. At this point, Runt realizes he's hungry and remembers that he's hid some snacks around town. He's not ready to go on without them, since who knows how much energy Chicken Little's problems will take up?

When the friends' conversation is finished, three locations pop up over the northwest side of town and you're given 50 seconds to collect all three snacks. There's an arrow pointing at each snack, and beacons appear from far away. Watch the mini-map to choose the closest one, and move toward it. When you approach the middle location from the southeast, check the backyards next to it and directly in the center of town to pick up two of the five **cards** hidden around town. When you see a clock icon, pick it up and add its time to your limit.

Once you've grabbed the last snack, it's time for the first of a chain of non-timed errands. Drive to the northwest corner of the map to pick up a stack of surfboards propped against a house. Drive straight into them and they're automatically loaded onto your car. Now you have four more locations scattered around town where you need to drop them off. Drive into the glowing red areas beside the houses to unload each surfboard in turn.

Your next target after the papers is back near the center of town. You must pick up a wooden **trough**, which is loaded onto the top of your car as soon as you touch it. Four more locations appear on the mini-map. These are baskets full of groceries for Runt's family. Drive through each one to pick it up and put it into the trough. If you drive along the north road between the two northernmost locations, you can pick up another **card** on a hill overlooking the road. When the trough is full, a dot appears back at its original location. Go back to drop off the now-full container.

With the surfboards all distributed, you need to pick up three magazines around town to get some helpful tips for Chicken Little's situation. When you pick up the southernmost magazine in front of a courthouse, drive northwest to find a third **card** beside the sliding board in a playground. When you're finished reading the articles, go back to the southeast to pick up a bundle of newspapers for delivery.

Now it's back to the northwest to pick up a platter of food. When you collect the platter, it kicks off another timed errand. This time, you have 60 seconds to throw the food at five houses. This time, the deliveries fly straight ahead from the front of the car.

Knowing the best routes is more important now, because the quickest way between some of the far-flung locations isn't a straight line. Pick off the house to the southwest first. Then swing up to deliver to the three center locations at the same time, picking up the two time extensions from the yards if you see them on your way past. Follow the road and swing around to reach the southeast location from the north side. Pick up the last **card** behind the house as soon as you finish your delivery.

## Speedy Delivery

Now you need to deliver the papers. Drive to each of the houses marked on the mini-map, and throw the papers toward the targets. You have unlimited throws, so don't worry about a miss. The paper comes out from the left front of the car, so aim as best you can. When you strike the target or the red area around the house, the target disappears and you move on to the next.

Once you're finished delivering, Chicken Little's house is just across the street from the last location. Drive into the red glow surrounding the house, and your errands are finished. Now it's time to see what the Misfits' friend has found.

29

# Backyard Pursuit

With his friends at his side, Chicken Little tries to figure out what the strange object that fell into his room might be. Fish-Out-of-Water gets a bit carried away—literally—when he uses the floating Hex panel to ride on and is whisked away into the distance. Naturally, Chicken Little and the others must follow their friend to make sure nothing happens to him! Guide Chicken Little through the backyards of the town, in pursuit of the beam of light, in hopes of rescuing Fish.

## PS2

 Jump
 Double Jump
Yo-yo Attack
Pole Climb
Yo-yo Swing
(Held) Powershot (After picking up the Powershot Upgrade)
Grapple

## GC

 Jump
 Double Jump
Yo-yo Attack
Pole Climb
Yo-yo Swing
(Held) Powershot (After picking up the Powershot Upgrade)
Grapple

## XBOX

 Jump
 Double Jump
Yo-yo Attack
Pole Climb
Yo-yo Swing
(Held) Powershot (After picking up the Powershot Upgrade)
Grapple

## ITEMS

**Powershot Upgrade**
Pick this up to power up your attacks and make them stronger.

## DANGERS

The Chicken Little toys are back on the rampage. Don't fall victim to their attacks!

Jump over the barricades on the various pipe-slides you take in your journey.

Don't fall into the river at any point.

Switch between pipes as necessary during the final pipe-slide segment, or else you'll fall into the water.

## Backyard Destruction

You'll need a bit of extra power on your side to run through the other yards in hot pursuit. As soon as the mission starts, run forward to grab the new yo-yo in the yard. This is a Powershot Upgrade. You can power up your attacks by holding down and then releasing it.

Run forward to reach the gate, which is surrounded by a strange blue glow. This glow marks objects that you must destroy with your new powered-up yo-yo. Move right up next to the gate and do a Powershot. The gate falls to pieces and you're free to move into the next yard.

Over to the left of this yard, you find a garage door also marked by the blue glow. Break it open and run inside, and you find another carton of the Chicken Little toys. With your stronger yo-yo, you can charge a Powershot next to one of these cartons to destroy it. This way no more toys can come after you.

With the dangerous toys out of the way, move to the left side of the garage and use a normal attack to break two boxes stacked together. The board that they were holding up drops down. Run up this board onto a plank high in the garage, where you find your first **card** for the chapter.

Now jump back down to the ground and run under the plank that held the card, destroying some sacks of acorns to continue through the back of the garage. The path here curves around to the next yard, where you find a Chicken Little toy. Destroy it, and then move up to use a Powershot on the bit of fence at the end of the path. With the fence gone, run into the yard.

Before you move toward the next yard, destroy the carton of toys next to the house, fighting off any toys that escape in the process. Now climb the ladder on the sliding board in the center of the yard by double-jumping between the rungs. When you reach the top, step forward to slide down the board. You're thrown forward through the air to fly through a tire swing, collecting the second **card** on the way.

To the left of your landing spot is another garage door. Break it open with a powered-up attack. This causes a ledge on top of the door to fall down and lock into place. Inside the garage are a few items you can break open for acorns, along with a Chicken Little toy.

When you're done in the garage, go to the corner of the house to find a box on the ground. Jump onto it, jump up, and pull yourself up onto a windowsill. From the windowsill, grab onto a pipe leading up and jump from the top onto the roof.

Find the other pipe leading up, and climb it until you can jump to a white ledge. Start from the side of the pipe closest to the ledge, and you may have to double-jump if you miss your target at first. From the center of the ledge, double-jump straight up and latch onto the cable. Then slide down to the ledge over the garage door.

From one corner of the ledge, you see a trampoline nearby. Double-jump in that direction to land on the trampoline, and then bounce up high and move over the fence into the next yard. Here you must fight off a few Chicken Little toys and break another of their crates tucked away at the side of the yard, under a roof. When the box is gone, power-up your yo-yo and break the wooden support in the center, and another ledge falls down into place.

On the right side of this roofed area, jump up onto the box, leap up onto the ledge, and then make a left turn onto the connected boards. From the end of this second ledge, grapple to a pipe on the house, pulling yourself up to a small platform. From the corner of this platform, climb up a pipe to jump onto the roof of the house.

## Pool Party

Up on the roof, you have one more pipe to climb, and then you slide down a cable into a small fenced-in area. Break open the blue glowing gate to reach the yard of a lucky family with a pool. Break the wooden support at ground level to drop down the end of a board. Then climb the slope, but watch out for the Chicken Little toys roaming the yard.

When you're done fighting, run up the board and destroy the next wooden support to lower another plank. Go up again to reach the pool's surface. Move to the other side of the water to find two pipes. First climb the one to the left. It seems to lead nowhere, but if you time a jump or double-jump just right and face toward the house, you can throw out a grapple at the top of your jump to latch onto a hook and pull yourself up to the house. Once you're on the ledge at the front of the building, pick up the **card** before jumping back down to the pool.

From the pool, climb the pipe to the right. This leads up to a cable, which you slide down to reach one more yard. At the bottom of the cable is another box of toys for you to quickly dispatch. Next, run over to another garage door and break it open, fighting the toy that runs toward you from inside. If you need more acorns, collect them from the breakable objects past the doors. Then head back outside.

Back out in the yard, jump onto a picnic table, and then face the house until you see the prompt to use the grapple. Pull yourself over to a platform beside the house, and climb the pipe and jump from the top onto the awning. This acts as another trampoline. Move carefully toward the opposite edge of the awning. At the height of your bounce, double-jump over to the lower ledge on one side of the garage.

Once you reach the ledge, follow it along each wall and jump out onto the ledge above where the garage doors were. Here you find yet another pipe to climb, which leads to a cable that slides you onto another wooden structure.

# Out and Away

Now you're reaching the edge of the backyards and heading into the countryside. Climb up the pipe to reach the top of the structure, and collect any acorns you need from the breakable containers. When you're ready, drop into the open drain. It's a waterslide! Follow it down the pipe and out onto a wooden platform, where you reach a checkpoint.

From the checkpoint, climb up the boards and jump to a second set of boards, pulling yourself up and onto the water bank. Be careful, because there's a Chicken Little toy waiting here for you. Destroy it, and then use a Powershot to destroy the wooden support and drop another board within your reach.

Go up the board, and then jump from ledge to ledge around the water tower. When you reach the end of one ledge, climb the pipe and slide down the cable at the top to reach a cliff. Destroy the rocks in front of you with another Powershot. Then run forward, double-jump from the cliff onto two stone platforms that tilt if you stand on them for too long, and then double-jump to another cliff.

From the opposite edge of this second cliff, jump out, grab onto a branch, then swing across to a third cliff. Destroy the dead tree at the opposite end. Cross the wooden bridge to jump onto a pipe-slide, jumping over the usual barricades along the way.

When you reach the bottom of the slide, run forward and to the right to use your Powershot on a wooden log. With this log gone, a gear starts to turn, opening the cover of a grate nearby. Now cross over the wooden bridge and do the same thing to trigger a second gear.

With both covers open, go to the middle of the wooden bridge and face toward the water. When you're at the right spot and facing in the right angle, the prompt appears. Use your grapple to pull yourself over to a grate in the middle of the water. Turn to face another grate, use your grapple again, and finish up with a third grapple to take you over to the grates themselves.

Pick up a **card** from the left-hand open grate. To clean up after yourself or get an extra acorn or two, go into the right grate and destroy the Chicken Little toy inside it. Then collect the acorns. Now continue over to the right of that grate to use a Powershot on one more log holding back a gear, which opens the center grate.

Once the middle pipe is open, enter it and fight off the Chicken Little toy on your way in. Now step forward to go down yet another waterslide to a stepping stone in a river, as well as a handy checkpoint.

# Waterway Woes

With two quick double-jumps, make your way from one stepping stone to the next and then away from the water. Follow the trail of acorns up and around to the top of the small nearby hill, fighting two Chicken Little toys on the way. Now you've got a chain of fairly challenging feats to perform, so concentrate and put your skills to good use.

At the top of the hill, stand on the bit of broken bridge and face the river to use your grapple. This pulls you over to a rickety wooden platform, and also triggers the prompt. This platform collapses not long after you land on it. As soon as your feet touch the boards, run forward to the edge, double-jump off, and latch onto the next pole and swing from it. If you miss your timing, you're dumped back down to the ground below. That's not a big problem for now, but soon any missteps will become more serious.

When you swing back and forth from the pole, press the button when you're farthest out. You fly over to a bit of raised ground that you couldn't reach from below. Follow this trail down to a cluster of rocks, and use a Powershot to clear them out of your way. Run down to the river's edge and jump onto the rock just off the bank. Watch the leaves carefully.

Now you must time a jump carefully to land on one of the leaves floating by, without overshooting. This is where things get rough. If you fall into the water at this point, you go back to the checkpoint on the first of the stepping stones and have to start the sequence over. So time your jump well. A single jump is usually best here, if you leap while the leaf is very close to the stone.

When you make your jump just right, you float down the stream on a leaf, but don't get too comfortable just yet. Just down the river is a rock, with a pair of branches blocking the water beyond. Jump to the rock when the leaf gets close enough. Then stand on the edge closest to the branches and use a Powershot to clear the way.

33

Once the brush is out of the way, double-jump to the next stone, then double-jump again to another leaf passing by. Float on it a bit farther downstream. If you fall into the water and have to come back, don't make the mistake of riding the same leaf past the now-clear area between the rocks. The leaves drop down under the water at this point, dipping you into the river and sending you back to square one. Also keep in mind that if you lose all of your eggs, you're sent back to the very same point—but without any of the progress you've made, such as branches cleared out of the way.

Just beyond the first river blockage, you find the very same setup again. Clear the branches out of the way as before, and jump again from the second stone to a leaf to continue your journey, but only for a very short distance. Just past the second set of branches, you come to two rocks, one on each side of a waterfall. If you fall down this, you're submerged and sent back. Leap to the left-hand rock before you reach the waterfall.

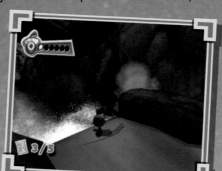

After crossing the second gap, leap up to grab onto a pole with your yo-yo. Then swing over the remainder of the rotten bridge, landing safely on the opposite bank. From here, run along the trail to fight another of the toys. Then jump across to a stone in the center of the river, which has a checkpoint. Whew!

From the rock, send out your grapple downstream to pull yourself over to the start of a pipe-slide. Slide down, watching carefully for barricades to jump and places where two new pipes start to run beside your own. Whenever you see these two pipes, it means that your own pipe is just about to end and dump you into the river. Jump and press toward one of the other pipes to switch over mid-slide.

## A Hop, a Skip, and a Jump

Once you're on the rock, turn to face downstream. When you face just the right direction, the grapple prompt appears on the screen. Grapple your way from the rock to another stone in the center of the stream. Unfortunately, this new rock is another unstable platform that starts to tilt. It falls shortly after you land, so quickly run to the edge and leap off, with a double-jump if necessary. Latch onto a nearby pipe, using a yo-yo swing.

For your first trip, at least, jump to the left pipe at the first switch, and then jump to the right. This takes you to the final **card** hanging over a barricade ending that slide. Of course, chances are that you'll fall into the river, but this only sends you back to the start of the pipe slides. If you miss the card on your first trip and make it to the bottom, you can simply stroll back into the river to go back to the checkpoint at the start of the slide.

From the first pipe, jump off at the height of your swing and latch onto the second pipe. From here, swing forward onto another of the tilting rocks, and jump from here to a high-up riverbank. Follow the trail to fight a Chicken Little toy. Then carefully cross the wooden bridge, jumping over the empty spaces where some of the boards have rotted away. Make sure you keep moving—just seconds after you land on the center of the bridge, the planks drop away under your feet. So make your double-jump across, run farther after landing, and start the next jump immediately.

Once you reach the end of the series of pipes, you have a gauntlet of three Chicken Little toys to fight your way through. With these out of the way, Powershot your way through another set of branches, and finally go out into the field.

# Space Simulator

They may have thought things were weird before, but Chicken Little and friends haven't seen anything yet! It turns out that the object that fell on Chicken Little was actually from a real, honest-to-goodness flying saucer, and the aliens have left to explore the town itself! At least this gives the friends a chance to try to save Fish, who is inside the heart of the UFO. But to gain entrance to the spacecraft, Chicken Little must pass a pilot simulation test with flying colors. Help him beat the machine, and get his friends inside!

Walkthrough

## PS2

| | |
|---|---|
| ⊗ | Thrust |
| □ | Shoot |
| □ | (Held) Continuously fire shots (while a Rapid Fire Pickup is active) |
| △ | Missile (while Missile Pickup is active) |
| L1 | Tilt Left |
| R1 | Tilt Right |

## GC

| | |
|---|---|
| A | Thrust |
| B | Shoot |
| B | (Held) Continuously fire shots (while a Rapid Fire Pickup is active) |
| Y | Missile (while Missile Pickup is active) |
| L | Tilt Left |
| R | Tilt Right |

## XBOX

| | |
|---|---|
| ⊗ | Thrust |
| ⊗ | Shoot |
| ⊗ | (Held) Continuously fire shots (while a Rapid Fire Pickup is active) |
| ⊗ | Missile (while Missile Pickup is active) |
| L | Tilt Left |
| R | Tilt Right |

## ITEMS

**Health Pickup**
Restore some health to a damaged craft

**Rapid Fire Pickup**
For a limited time allows you to continuously fire shots.

**Missile Pickup**
Allows you to fire missiles.

**Shield Pickup**
Gives you extra shielding for a short period of time.

## DANGERS

Avoid flying into any objects or debris.

Avoid enemy spaceships, including their fire.

## Test of Mettle

Although it may be from beyond the stars, the Space Simulator plays a lot like some of the video games from the past, which helps give Chicken Little a leg up on the program. In this simulator you are piloting a spaceship that can move up and down, left and right, but which keeps moving constantly forward at the same time, although you can accelerate by pressing a button. You must avoid solid objects and enemies, as well as enemy fire, but you can pick up a few handy upgrades along the way.

To check the various stats of your ship, look at the display in the top left corner of the screen. The bar at the top next to the heart icon displays your ship's current health. The first number below that is the number of missiles you have in stock, followed by the number of gates you've traveled directly through. The next meter going diagonally from bottom left to top right shows your remaining thrust, which refills slowly as you fly without using more. Icons below that show what pickups you have in effect, such as rapid fire or shielding.

The first object to come into view is a red heart-shaped icon, one of the health pickups that restores lost health to your ship. You don't really need it now, not having taken any damage. Directly after it the asteroids start to show up. Either dodge around them or shoot them out of the way—shooting them down is usually better as shooting objects may also release pickups. Asteroids usually have a chance to release a health pickup, although you shouldn't need one quite yet.

35

Just after a few of the asteroids, a green rapid fire pickup appears in the center of the screen, more useful than the last pickup for the moment. While this pickup only remains active for a short while, it lets you hold down the Shoot button to keep firing in a steady stream. After dodging a few more asteroids, a blue missile pickup shows up in the center, again a bit more useful than the first health pickup. This adds 10 missiles to your supply, giving you some heavier firepower than your normal shots.

Now you start to reach a land mass, which adds some new danger. There are now towers and other structures along the ground that you must dodge around, or destroy before you fly into them. When you blow up the towers, many of them provide you with an extra rapid fire pickup to keep your fire flowing, and just after the first tower a shield pickup appears in the center of the action to give you extra shielding over a short period of time. Two towers later you find a **card** near the center of the screen in front of the first of ten gates, so make sure you're in position to grab it as you fly by.

After avoiding the enemies and navigating a field of asteroids in open space, you go back to flying over the land, with plenty of structures to avoid or blow up as you fly past. This includes a **card** to the lower right quickly followed by a health pickup to the lower left, each in front of a gate. A tower comes next, with another mine to the right next to a fourth **card** to the left. Try to avoid a pair of turrets right after, with a handy health pickup in front of one last gate next to a tower before open space again.

In this one final stretch of open space another horde of enemies flies past while you have to blow your way through multiple asteroids, to keep from losing health on impact. Watch for the next gate as well, holding the final **card** shortly after you leave the land. There are two more gates, each with a health pickup, that show up around the same time as a second wave of enemies, to help keep you going to the end.

Just after the card shoot open a mine floating in space to uncover a missile pickup. Even if you don't need the missiles, mines drift directly toward your ship before blowing up, so take them out before that happens. After passing a turret that fires upon your ship you find another **card** to the lower right in front of another gate.

As you fly through this final stretch you eventually see a black and white checked line floating closer. This is the finish line, and once you reach the goal your objective is complete, and Chicken Little and friends can get inside the spacecraft, all thanks to his video game skills.

You soon float off the ground and back into open space, where you are greeted by enemies for you to shoot down while avoiding their own firepower. Don't be so overwhelmed by them that you miss a health pickup at the lower part of the screen in front of a third gate, partway through the trip through open space. Watch out for another mine just before the next land mass.

# Alien Abby

Chicken and his friends are now inside the flying saucer, but it's not quite what they'd expected. Just after stepping inside the group is separated by the defensive mechanisms, and now each character must find his or her own way through the ship! First up is Abby, who you must guide through the spacecraft in search of not only Fish, but now her two other missing friends.

## DANGERS

Don't fall from a great height!

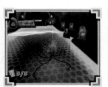
Shut down the generators to the energy barriers before trying to step through in your alien walker.

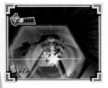
Watch out for the laser beams guarding some sections of a hall. Run through the openings and don't touch the beams.

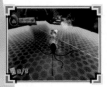
Avoid the laser fire of the patrol drones.

Be careful with the red boxes, and get away when they start to count down before they explode.

## PS2

| | |
|---|---|
| | Jump |
| | Double Jump |
| | Slingshot (hold to aim, release to shoot) |
| (Near an alien walker) | Enter alien walker |
| | Yo-yo Attack |
| (held) | Powershot |

**Alien Walker Controls:**

| | |
|---|---|
| | Enter and Exit Walker |
| R | Rotate top of Walker |
| L | Move Alien Walker |
| R1 | Fire Cannon |
| L1 | Pick up Object |

## GC

| | |
|---|---|
| | Jump |
| | Double Jump |
| | Slingshot (hold to aim, release to shoot) |
| (Near an alien walker) | Enter alien walker |
| | Yo-yo Attack |
| (held) | Powershot |

**Alien Walker Controls:**

| | |
|---|---|
| | Enter and Exit Walker |
| | Rotate top of walker |
| | Move Alien Walker |
| | Fire Cannon |
| | Pick up Object |

## XBOX

| | |
|---|---|
| | Jump |
| | Double Jump |
| | Slingshot (hold to aim, release to shoot) |
| (Near an alien walker) | Enter alien walker |
| | Yo-yo Attack |
| (held) | Powershot |

**Alien Walker Controls:**

| | |
|---|---|
| | Enter and Exit Walker |
| R | Rotate top of walker |
| L | Move Alien Walker |
| R | Fire Cannon |
| L | Pick up Object |

## ITEMS

**Alien Walker**
You can enter and exit these alien vehicles to make it to places unreachable by Abby alone.

**Health Pickup**
Find one of these icons inside a crate and touch it to restore some of the damages to your alien walker.

## Light As a Feather

Along with the ability to jump and double-jump like Chicken Little, Abby has one extra related ability. At the height of a jump or double-jump, Abby can float. This is useful for getting over wider gaps, where you can double-jump forward part of the way, then float down the rest. It's also good if you miss your target slightly on normal double-jumps, letting you float down to safety if you hit it quick enough.

Abby starts out on a raised surface surrounded by transparent platforms, each of which holds a few acorns. Jump around to each section of platform to collect the goods, then return to the platform and run forward to jump onto a switch. Stay on the switch until it fully unlocks the door and then run through, jumping to get into the portal.

Once past the doorway you have a straight hallway ahead, with a few more jumps along the way to get past raised areas. The next room holds a checkpoint, and another switch. As soon as you jump onto this switch a series of the transparent platforms appears, and a timer starts to count down in the top right corner of the screen. When the timer runs out the platform disappears, so jump your way across as quickly as you can, triggering a second checkpoint as you reach the next bit of solid ground on the other side.

Head through the next section of hallway to reach a room with exits in four directions. The doorway in front is blocked, and the one to the back is the direction you just came in, so your choices are between left and right. Go through the left doorway first, and run through another hallway to reach a room with a checkpoint and two switches, yellow and blue.

Jump on the yellow switch to bring up a series of yellow floating platforms leading around the room, and another timer at the top right. Jump along the platforms, collecting acorns as you go, and at the end you reach one final platform that holds a **card** on one end. Grab it, and run and jump your way back along the same path that you just came before the time runs out.

Once you're back to the start and the platforms vanish, jump onto the blue switch this time to trigger a new set of platforms. Now jump along the chain of platforms leading counterclockwise, steadily higher, to reach a second **card** toward the end of the chain. Turn to the left after you grab the card and double-jump from that corner of the platform back toward the original solid ground, and float back down to safety.

Now return to the intersection and take the other exit. Be careful as you start through the hall. Here new security starts to show up—lasers that move slowly across one section of the hall. Watch any lasers carefully as they move, and run through when there's an opening large enough for Abby and the lasers are still moving away. This particular laser shows up alone, and is slow-moving and easy to avoid, but this won't always be the case.

Through this next hallway you trigger another checkpoint. Double-jump from the edge of the solid floor and float over to the next section in the center of the room. Here jump on a switch to unlock the last door in the intersection. Double-jump and float back to the safe ground, and take the hallway back to the newly-unlocked door.

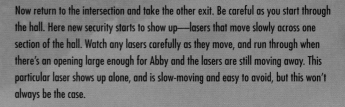

Head through the now open doorway which is lit up in green, avoiding a pair of lasers this time. In the next room you find a checkpoint hovering over a strange contraption. Get close enough to trigger the checkpoint, then enter the alien walker.

# Out For a Stroll

In this alien walker you have a new set of controls to learn and use. You move the vehicle around the room with normal movement controls, but in this case the camera and facing of the walker don't change as you move. To swivel these around to different directions you need to use the right analog stick. You also have two different weapons, a laser beam and a tractor beam. The one you should use right now is the laser beam.

At the side of the room is a sealed door with four red lights around it, two on each side. The bottom two lights are switches, while the top lights show whether or not the light's "linked" switch has been triggered. Fire a laser beam directly at the bottom lights and they each turn from red to green, with the top lights changing to green as the bottom lights change. The door slides open when you trigger both switches.

Enter the next room and watch out for a patrol drone shaped like a globe that floats around a bit past the doorway. Fire on it with your laser beam before it can fire at you. If you start to take damage, watch the bar in the upper-left corner of the screen. This is your walker's health bar, and if it reaches zero it has the same effect as if you'd run out of eggs with a normal character.

With the patrol drone out of the way turn your attention to the sealed door. Trigger the switches as you did with the first door, and if necessary pick up the box sitting on the floor to move it out of the way, then pressing the laser button to throw it. Sometimes when you destroy a box it releases a health pickup to restore some of your walker's health, so if you've taken some hits smash open a few boxes whenever you're safe from attack.

In the next section you have a pair of the drones to destroy, although you may have to move some of the boxes out of the way first. Keep moving to avoid being a stationary target while you get the crates out of your path of fire. With these drones down, just around the corner more are waiting to attack, so be ready with your laser beam. This time the actual switches for the door are off to the sides of the hall, one behind a few more of the boxes that you need to move aside.

Now past this last door, things get a bit more hectic for a while. You enter a more open room full of patrol drones, some of them off the sides of the platform firing in upon your walker. Keep moving and strafe the entire area with laser fire, cutting down the drones as quickly as possible to minimize the damage you take.

Even after you start cutting down the drones within the room reinforcements appear from the portals to the sides of the platform and from the opposite door periodically, although after each spitting out a few more of the drones they too finally stop. Once you've taken out all of the original droids and any that are sent in after the fight starts, the doors slide open, allowing you to continue on your way. If you've taken a lot of damage in the previous fight try breaking open any remaining boxes by throwing them against the door or another object, to see if any drop the health pickups.

Through the next door you find metallic objects on the ground, surrounded by pulsing red lights. Walk in between these objects, making sure not to touch them or the lights surrounding them. These are alien mines, and if you come too close they leap up, explode, and damage your craft. It's a bit of a narrow squeeze, but you can just get your walker in between mines without setting them off. If you do accidentally touch one, try backing up quickly—sometimes you can trigger them and back up before they explode, avoiding damage.

Just past this section of corridor is one of the "landing pads" for the alien walkers. Approach the circle in the center of the room to let Abby get back on her own two webbed feet.

# Take a Hike

Run through the next person-sized door and avoid two more lasers, the first going side to side, the next going between top and bottom. The next room is another four-way intersection with the front portal sealed, so turn left and run through a hallway to a room with a new checkpoint.

Once you trigger the checkpoint, look ahead and to the right to find a transparent platform rising from a base. After it reaches a certain height, the platform flickers and vanishes. Jump to one of these platforms as it starts its trip upward, and at its highest point before it vanishes double-jump toward the next similar platform, floating the extra distance. If you stand still on the platform you'll just drop straight down when it disappears without taking any harm, so ride a few platforms first to get a good idea of how high they go before making the leap.

From the second base and rising platform, fly your way over to a third in the same way, but on the third platform make certain you ride it high enough to collect a **card** high up in the air. Just after the card you collect an acorn, which is a warning that the platform is about at its highest point. Jump on to the next platform in the chain which is also the first platform you rode, and from there back to the first bit of solid flooring.

Now run back to the intersection of hallways, and this time take the one that was originally to the right, straight ahead from where you're currently coming out. You pass a set of lasers with one moving up and down, one moving side to side, and run into a room with another checkpoint, and one more of the clear rising platforms.

This time the clear platform doesn't rise nearly as high, so ride it a few times to get a good idea of its highest point, then double-jump and float from there to the more solid platform on the other side of the room. Jump onto the switch in the center to open the last door in the intersection, then make your way back to that open doorway. On the way back, make sure you grab another **card** that's floating in the air while jumping from the rising platform back to the original bit of solid ground.

Run through the open door, and be very careful going past the next grid of lasers which has three beams to avoid. In the next room jump on a switch to bring up a series of platforms, along with another timer. Go to the right and jump between the platforms and continue to the end of the room to pick up the last **card** before turning to one of the rising platforms. Grabbing the card may not give you enough time to then jump to the solid platform, but an egg is usually a fair trade for one of the few cards on the level.

Once on the round platform in the center of the room ride the rising platform that appears, then again jump from one platform to the next back the way you came in a chain leading to another piece of solid flooring above the first, and a handy checkpoint. After you trigger the checkpoint run through the door and dodge your way through a string of laser-guarded points until you reach one more room with a checkpoint.

Now jump on the switch at the end of your current ledge to open a door on the floor below. Enter the alien walker before heading through that very same door, toward the end of the level.

# Back in the Saddle

With Abby once more in the driver's seat of an alien walker, move forward into the next block-filled room. Here there are a few red-colored boxes in amongst the green, and you must be wary of them. If you start to lift them, or disturb them too much, they start to make noise as a sort of countdown. After a few seconds and two higher-pitched tones one last tone shifts down in pitch and the box explodes, damaging anyone or anything nearby. You can however use them as a sort of weapon to throw at any nearby patrol drones, if you're careful.

Make your way carefully through this section and through the sliding door into a portion of the hall with patrol drones firing upon you. Blow them up with your laser beam or with one of the red crates, and watch out for a few more drones that appear from holes in the wall. When the hall is clear and no more drones show up turn and trigger the right-hand switch beside the next door, then fire upon the next switch back at the corner, off at a distance beyond the wall. With both switches triggered, the door slides open as usual.

If you have trouble getting the shield to actually explode, it helps to wait for the block's "countdown" to reach the end just as you throw it; so listen for the shift in tone and then launch. This lets the block hit the shield just as it explodes. The wide-open shields like this one usually aren't so picky; but some of the other shield puzzles may require a more delicate touch.

The next section holds another patrol drone, but it's not the only danger found here. There is also a barrier of energy stretched across the hallway. Fire upon the patrol drone from a distance to destroy it, then approach the barrier, but don't touch it! Get too close and you damage your craft as it takes a nasty jolt.

Now walk past and start to fire upon more of the patrol drones both around the corner and starting to appear from more holes in the walls of the hallway. Destroy them until no more appear, but be careful of a second pair of red blocks at this further end of the hall section. You may also have to move around the normal green blocks to get a clear shot at some of the foes.

From a point near the barrier turn your camera left to find a glowing green generator off to the side. Fire upon this with your lasers, and once it has been destroyed the barrier disappears. You do still have to be careful as such barriers may still throw out a quick surge of energy from time to time, but just after knocking this one down you can quickly step through without taking damage.

Once the drones are gone for good, look to the left and right sides of the hall. You find one switch for the door on each side, each covered with a shield. Make sure you clear the objects out from in front of the left-hand switch first, as otherwise you might accidentally blow the red crate up when it strikes them, causing it to explode closely enough that it damages your craft. Now grab the red box, swing it around, and throw it into the shield before it explodes. You may have to move back and forth a bit to be able to both pick up the box and get it launched far enough toward the shield to connect. Once the shield detonates you are free to trigger the switch.

The switches to the next door are both just beside the closed doorway, so blast them to unlock the door and enter the next area. Here you find a few dangers clustered close together—a red block is off to the right inside a device that replaces the block whenever it blows up. Just beyond that is another energy barrier, with patrol drones further past it. First stand back and pick off the drones, then turn your attention to the barrier.

This time turn to your right to find two generators off to the side, one covered by a purple shield. Blow up the normal one with your laser, then you need to pick up the red block and throw it directly into the shield around the other generator before it explodes. If you hit the shield dead center with the block as it blows up, giving you access to the generator itself. Now blow up the generator with your laser, shutting down the energy barrier in the hallway.

With the first switch cleared, turn back to the right and work on this side. It's the same basic idea, but this time you have to time your throw right and aim it well so that it sails between two metal plates that slam together and then move apart in front of the switch. This takes a bit of practice, but be patient and you'll get the timing down. You may also need to worry more about timing the throw right on both of these puzzles to allow the explosion to occur just as the crate reaches the shield, which makes it even more tricky to get the door open.

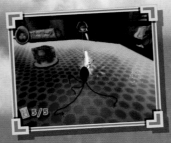

Once you trigger both switches walk through the open door. Here you run into another small swarm of patrol drones, with a red box in the center to be wary of. Run in circles around the box and fire off to the sides to take out the multiple drones, and listen for the tones that mean the box has been set off, so you can move away in time. Once the patrol drones are all gone the door behind you re-opens, but you want to move forward. Now turn your attentions to the rest of the room.

From the left side of where you first entered the room you find two shielded generators. As before you need to pick up the box and throw it into each of the two shields. The trick this time is that there's a bit of a distance between the box and the shields, so you have

to do a bit more walking between where you pick up the box and the edge of the platform where you throw it, to make sure you clear the railing around the platform.

It takes a bit of practice again, but after two successful throws and two follow-up shots the generators are destroyed and the energy barrier to one end of the room vanishes. Be a bit more careful about the barrier's surges this time, since it's a slight distance off and you can't just move past immediately after destroying the generators. Once the flickering dies down temporarily, walk past the next doorway to hit a checkpoint and exit your walker, then run through the small doorway out of the room. You run through a hall and into a new room, jump down to the floor below, and voila—your mission is complete.

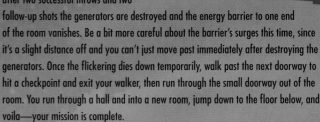

# Runaway Runt

With Abby safely at her destination, it's Runt's turn to take the spotlight. Unfortunately, he has problems that Abby didn't. When he got separated from his friends, he ended up on a runaway trip, going down the hall upside down! Direct Runt's slide as best you can to help him reach his friends in one piece.

## PS2

 Jump
Shoot (Only with Missile Pickup)

## GC

 Move left and right
Jump
Shoot

## XBOX

 Move left and right
Jump
Shoot

## ITEMS

Missile Pickup
Recharge your maximum supply of eight missiles.

## DANGERS

Avoid striking the green or dark blue boxes.

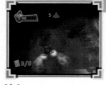

Make sure you open every door before running into it, or you have to start over.

Jump over or slide around the various bars of energy, or lose an egg.

Slide around the red pillars, or you'll have to start over.

## Unstoppable Slide

Runt's got his head stuck in an alien pail and is sliding quickly down the hall, so all you can do is move him right and left around objects. You cannot make him go faster or slow him down. In a pinch, you can fire missiles to clear things out of your way, but these are very limited in number. You should try to save them as much as possible.

You start out with no missiles, sliding down the center of the hall. There are two types of dangers to watch out for. Some objects are less solid than others and take away one of your eggs if you connect from the side. Other objects are more solid and stop your slide completely, forcing you to start over from the beginning of the slide with your three eggs. There are no checkpoints during this slide. You either make it through the entire thing without losing all of your eggs, or you don't.

Because your eggs are so precious with no checkpoints available, collect as many acorns as you can on your way down the hall. Don't let yourself lose an egg trying to grab just one difficult acorn, but at the same time, pick up as many as you think you can safely grab.

The first thing you see sliding toward you in the center of the hall is a dark blue box, with taller green boxes behind it and to the sides. If you hit a box, you lose one egg regardless of color.

Whenever you have to hit switches like this, make sure you do it as soon as possible. The missiles hit from a surprising distance, and it takes a moment for the door to open. If you hit the switch at the last minute, it doesn't open in time and you crash into it, taking you directly back to the start of the slide.

Slide around the first dark box and skirt around the next two green boxes, but make sure that you're sliding over behind the right-hand box as it goes past. There's a hidden **card** behind it. Then slide quickly over to the center, just missing the next green box, to grab a Missile Pickup.

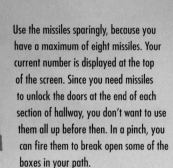

## Behind Door Number One

As soon as you enter the second section, you're faced with more trouble. Large red pillars that cannot be destroyed stretch from floor to ceiling, and hitting one of these takes you back to the start of the slide. Avoid the first one by sliding to either side. Then watch out for a blue box to the right, followed by a pillar to the left.

The next pillars are to the right and center, so you should slide toward the left after the last left-hand pillar. Stay there to jump over the next bar of energy, because there's a blue box to the right just behind it, but be ready to start sliding toward the right as you hit the ground. Just behind the box is another bar of energy that moves from side to side along the hallway, and you must gauge your position to slide through an empty space. It's usually better to slide through on one side, rather than down the center.

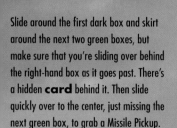

Use the missiles sparingly, because you have a maximum of eight missiles. Your current number is displayed at the top of the screen. Since you need missiles to unlock the doors at the end of each section of hallway, you don't want to use them all up before then. In a pinch, you can fire them to break open some of the boxes in your path.

Shortly after picking up the missiles, watch out for a dark blue box in the center of the hall. After you avoid this, you have a new danger to worry about. An energy barrier is stretched along the floor of the hall, and you must jump over it or lose an egg. After another green box and another blue one in the center of the hall, you have a second energy barrier to jump, and then a third.

Just after the vertical energy bar is another one stretched across the floor for you to jump, with a Missile Pickup in the center of the hall after it. This is followed shortly by another floor-based energy barrier. As you reach the end of the next section, there are triggers to the lower-right and lower-left of the door, with two boxes lined up in the center. Fire on one of the switches as soon as you can, and then slide across the hall between the two boxes to shoot a missile at the other. A second **card** is behind the box closest to the door, so make it over to the center in time to pick it up.

Swing into the center of the hall after jumping the third barrier, and pick up the second set of missiles if you need them. Watch out for the blue boxes on the right, and then in the center. Swing to the left of the last blue box, and use one of your missiles while sliding forward on the ground. This hits the switch next to the sliding door and opens it.

Stay in the center of the hall as the door slides open, and you're in line to pick up another set of missiles just inside. Then there's an energy bar to jump over, followed by a blue box to the right and another of the side-moving energy barriers to slide past. After you pass, jump over another horizontal energy barrier behind it.

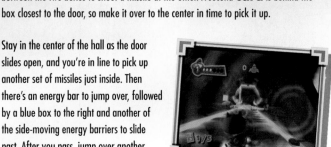

43

Now you have two more vertical bars of energy in a row, quickly moving from side to side. Do your best to judge which side will take you through both bars safely. The center is almost always a bad bet. Watch the green box on the right, which you might hit square-on if you're not careful. Then there's a blue box behind it in the center, followed by another energy bar along the floor to jump.

Slide to the right to grab another set of missiles, if you're running low, and slide left as soon as you grab them to avoid the green box. As you approach the next door, you have switches on the lower- and upper-right. On the right side of the hall, jump and fire at the top of your leap to unlock the higher door. Then fire again at the bottom. Move twice to the left as quickly as possible to grab the third **card** before soaring through the door. If you can't quite manage it, you might consider just picking up the card and making the sacrifice of going back to the beginning, depending on how important unlocking the mini-games is to you.

Just inside the door is another Missile Pickup in the center of the hall. It's quickly followed by three energy barriers in a row moving from side to side, making it even harder to judge the right place to go through each barrier. Take the first barrier as best you can on the fly after grabbing the missiles, and then try to judge the next two from there.

After a brief interval, you slide past a blue box in the center, followed by a red pillar also in the middle of the hall. Go by them to the right, since they're soon followed by a pair of pillars taking up the left side of the hall. Jump over an energy barrier, immediately swing to the center to pick up a set of missiles, and then swing left to be ready to jump over three more barriers in a row.

As you jump over the first or second bar, shoot off a missile at the top of your jump. Slide quickly over to the right side of the hall, jump the next barrier, and then shoot off another missile when you land. If you time these two missiles right, they should unlock the door shortly behind the third bar. Then you can slide on through after making your last jump.

Be ready to avoid a pillar on the left as you enter the next section. This is immediately followed by a pillar on the left alongside a pillar on the right, with a blue box between them. Shoot the box in the center, and slide through the middle of the hall between the pillars.

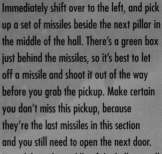

Immediately shift over to the left, and pick up a set of missiles beside the next pillar in the middle of the hall. There's a green box just behind the missiles, so it's best to let off a missile and shoot it out of the way before you grab the pickup. Make certain you don't miss this pickup, because they're the last missiles in this section and you still need to open the next door. Now slide to the middle of the hall as a pillar goes by to the right, and quickly slide in behind it to grab the fourth **card**.

This puts you in a position to slide past the next set of pillars that take up the left and center of the hall. Then slide to the left side to avoid the next set, along the right and center of the hall. You now must move far right, far left, and far right in quick succession to avoid the next three sets of pillars.

After the last set of pillars, start sliding toward the left again, jump over the bar of energy, and finish your left-slide to avoid another pair of pillars along the right side. Just as the pillars go by, slide back into the center to avoid a lone left-hand pillar. Then jump over the energy barrier along the floor. Move to one side or the other, and as you jump over the next bar, shoot off a missile to trigger one of the switches on the upcoming door.

When you land, slide to the other side of the hall, jump over the next bar, and shoot again to trigger the other switch. As you jump over one last barrier, slide to the center, blast the green box, and pick up the last **card** behind it. You're now ready to slide through the open doorway, which finally takes you to a hole leading to the center of the ship, and out of this chapter.

# Space Alarm

While the other friends are off having their own adventures, Chicken Little must also make his way to the center of the alien craft. Now it's his turn to be guided to safety through the halls and dangers inside the spaceship. Take him carefully through each obstacle to help him reach his friends at the end.

## PS2

| | |
|---|---|
| ⊗ | Jump |
| ⊗⊗ | Double Jump |
| ☐ | Yo-yo Attack |
| ☐ | Pole Climb |
| ☐ | Yo-yo Swing |
| △ (held) | Powershot |
| △ | Grapple |
| ○ | Slingshot (hold to aim, release to fire) (Requires the slingshot upgrade) |

## GC

| | |
|---|---|
| Ⓐ | Jump |
| ⒶⒶ | Double Jump |
| Ⓑ | Yo-yo Attack |
| Ⓑ | Pole Climb |
| Ⓑ | Yo-yo Swing |
| Ⓨ (held) | Powershot |
| Ⓨ | Grapple |
| Ⓧ | Slingshot (hold to aim, release to fire) (Requires the slingshot upgrade) |

## XBOX

| | |
|---|---|
| ○ | Jump |
| ○○ | Double Jump |
| ○ | Yo-yo Attack |
| ○ | Pole Climb |
| ○○ | Yo-yo Swing |
| ○ (held) | Powershot |
| ○ | Grapple |
| ○ | Slingshot (hold to aim, release to fire) (Requires the slingshot upgrade) |

## DANGERS

 Avoid the laser beams securing some parts of the hall.

 Watch out for the electric attacks of the mechanical guards.

 Leave the glowing globes of energy alone, or avoid their glass if you burst them open.

 Be careful of falling from high places.

 Don't stand on the lit platforms when they turn red.

 Watch out for any energy barriers you come across, and don't touch them.

 Don't let the drones get too close to your gun!

 Jump over the bars of light along the final pathway to safety.

## ITEMS

 **Slingshot Upgrade**
Pick this up to use the weapon to fire at far-off switches.

 **Battery**
Collect two of these to finish powering up the teleport device.

## Back to Basics

It might take you a while to get used to playing Chicken Little again, after having directed Abby around the ship and then taken control of Runt's mad slide, so test out your different controls if you need to and ease back into the role.

Run forward to navigate through a hallway, with one portal guarded by two lasers flowing from side to side and one moving up and down. Wait for an empty space to appear with the lasers preferably moving away from you, and squeeze through quickly.

45

Here you have a series of platforms to jump across, but there's a catch. The smaller platforms turn red from time to time, and whenever they're red they damage you. So before you jump onto the first platform wait for it to turn red, and then jump to it as soon as it becomes normal again. Run across and quickly jump to the large platform, which doesn't change color. On the large platform you find four domes of glass, each of which holds an acorn. Break them open and collect the acorns for a boost toward your next egg.

Go to the other side of the large platform, where two more of the smaller platforms sit in a row. Wait for the nearest one to turn red and then back to normal, then jump to it. The second platform is timed to turn normal just after the first, so if you jump to it quickly and then to the next large platform and checkpoint you don't have to worry about being caught by a red light. Like most of the large platforms in this area, this too holds a couple of the acorns under glass.

Now from this large platform jump to the next small one in the chain when it turns normal, and quickly turn toward the left and jump toward a floating object, latch on with your yo-yo and swing back and forth. When you're out farthest from the platform let go, and land on a new type of platform with a strange surface.

This new platform acts as a trampoline, sending Chicken Little high into the air after he lands on it. At the highest point in your bounce move forward toward the next platform, using an extra jump in mid-air if you have to cover a little more ground. From this large platform you have another small red platform to navigate, and another swing slightly to the right, this time onto another of the small red platforms. Time the release of your swing carefully to make sure you don't land on it when it's turning red.

From the small platform jump immediately to the larger one to trigger a checkpoint, and pick up the **card** over toward the left-hand side. From here jump over to solid ground, and enter the next hallway guarded by more of the slanted lasers. Through here you have yet another checkpoint before your next challenge.

As you enter the next room the door shuts behind you, and you are faced with a mechanical guard. Run right up to it and start attacking with your yo-yo—it usually takes three to four strikes to knock one of these out for the count, forcing it to drop an acorn. You can also charge one powershot as you run toward it, and take it out with one good hit.

The danger with these guards is that if they have a few seconds to home in on you they let loose an electric attack much like a lightning bolt, and if this strikes you, you lose an egg. This attack can strike at a distance, but not from clear across the room giving you some chance to dodge it.

When the first guard is gone, the room is bathed in a red light and another guard prepares its attack to the rear and left. It slides through the transparent "door" blocking its room and almost immediately lets loose its electricity attack. This means that you have two strategies depending on how close you are when a guard like this appears. If you get to the guard immediately as it comes into the room, start attacking so you can prevent its own attack. If you are at a bit of a distance get as far away as you can, then keep running in a circular path around the guard to keep away from its attack. After a few seconds the guard lets up on its attack and has to recharge, giving you the chance to move in and strike in turn.

Once both guards are gone the red light dies down and four rooms off of your current central room slide open. The door you arrived through remains closed, as does the door opposite, although the latter has a red switch over top of it. Enter each of the four side rooms and break open the clear domes holding more acorns. Inside one room just clockwise of the door with the switch you find a **card**, while the one clockwise of that holds a **slingshot** that you should pick up.

The slingshot upgrade itself is needed to navigate through much of this level, including getting you out of the central room. Return to the large circular room, stand in the middle and face the closed door. Press the Aim button and hold it down to aim the slingshot, and use your normal movement method to move the crosshairs around—in this case, pressing up moves the crosshairs down, and vice versa.

Once inside the next doorway you find another checkpoint, as well as another of the mechanical guardians. Now use the same method that you used in the first room of the chapter, destroying the first guard and then another that appears from the front right, this time destroying a third as well that appears from the rear left in order to open the side rooms. As before open the glass domes to collect the acorns, and pick up another **card** from behind one of the glowing orbs of energy before returning to the central chamber.

## If you shoot the orbs from the central chamber, it will break all the glass revealing acorns.

Walkthrough

Your target is the red switch over top of the closed doorway. Aim carefully, release the button to fire your shot right at the switch. If it connects, the switch turns to green and unlocks the door. You have unlimited ammunition so if you miss the first time just try again until you get it right.

This time there are two red switches instead of one, and they're inside the "doorway" instead of above it. Make sure you stand directly in the center of the room, then fire at one of the switches. Once you hit it a timer appears and you have a limited time to hit the other one as well, to turn them both green. If you don't hit the second before the timer runs out, you have to start again.

Once the door opens run through to reach another checkpoint. In this next room, more of the transparent disc platforms are floating around the area, this time moving downward. Jump to the closest one just as it drifts past, then turn to the right and start jumping and double-jumping along the chain of discs zig-zagging across the room. When you reach the end of the chain jump down to a solid platform in the center of the room.

Once both lights are green a clear disc rises from the center of the room and carries you upward. If you are standing too far to the edge and miss the disc another one will appear, but it takes a short while. As you ride the disc watch for a ledge to appear for you to jump onto, then run along it into the next room, holding another checkpoint.

From this platform find the doorway along the circular wall level with your platform, with yellow symbols around it and a red switch over top. Use your slingshot to hit this switch, and clear blue platforms appear between you and the door, along with a timer in the upper right corner of the screen. Immediately start jumping your way over to the doorway before the timer runs out.

Now you are faced with another switch in front of you, hanging at the center of the large open room. Use your slingshot again to trigger the switch, and more of the glowing discs appear and start moving down. Jump onto the one just ahead and to the right as it drifts down within reach, then jump and double-jump your way along this chain of discs as it curves around in an arc, to reach the next platform in the center. Ignore the doorway off to one side of the wall, as it may seem like your destination but is just too far off to reach.

Your next target is a doorway with red symbols around it and the usual red switch, just below the level of your platform. When you trigger the switch it causes more blue-tinted clear platforms to appear with the usual timer, this time gradually leading downward. Jump across them to the doorway, and enter to trigger the next checkpoint.

In the next hallway you find another portal guarded by lasers, this time moving at a slant across the circle. Move through an empty spot and enter another large room.

Turn toward the right and run up to the edge of the platform. Now there are two more platforms floating in circles around the next large open platform. Time your jump onto one of the moving plates very carefully, jumping out just as it is floating toward your position. From the floating platform jump onto the large platform in the center—don't take too long, or else the platform you're riding will swing into an energy barrier.

After you trigger the checkpoint on the platform run across to its opposite edge, and time your jump again to soar onto another floating platform. Run to the other side where you can just see a platform off across a gap, with an object sticking out of the center. Use your grapple to latch onto this object and pull yourself forward onto the next platform.

From the other side, leap onto another of the red-lit platforms once it's safe, then double-jump out to grab onto another swing with your yo-yo. At the far end of your swing release the object, and hit your Attack button again to latch onto the next swing. Now let go to soar over onto another large platform, with the next checkpoint.

# Strange Devices

After the next checkpoint you have a chain of three of the red-lit platforms to run along, ending in one of the trampoline-like platforms. Far above this platform is a swing to grab onto using your yo-yo. To reach it bounce multiple times in the same spot on the trampoline, to send you higher and higher. Wait until you are at your very highest peak in your jump from the trampoline, then if you still can't latch onto the swing hit the Jump button for an extra push in mid-air, giving you just enough height reach the device with your yo-yo.

Swing forward onto the large platform, and into another checkpoint. Now you have a series of three trampolines in a row—jump carefully from the first to the second, and then to the third. At the third trampoline you have another swing high up. Use the same method as before to reach it, and swing forward onto a small platform when its red light is gone. Quickly jump forward onto the large platform.

# Battery Power

In the center of the next platform are three strange devices. One already holds a battery inside—your job is to find the other two batteries and bring them back to the devices, to activate a teleporter ahead. Now look to each side of the platform, where you see two switches floating off in the distance.

Turn toward the left-hand switch and trigger it with your slingshot. Once you hit the switch another series of the transparent blue platforms appears, with the usual timer. Jump across the chain to reach a fourth **card**, along with a **battery**. The timer will run out at about this point but don't worry—you can reach another switch from this side with your slingshot, to bring the timed platforms back up.

Once you jump back across to the large platform, hit the switch on the right side, automatically placing the second battery into a device as you brush past. This time halfway along the platforms you collect the last **card** on your way, picking up the remaining **battery** when you get to the platform at the end of the chain. As before hit the switch closest to your platform once you pick up the battery, and follow the platforms back to the

Walk up next to the last device to place the third battery, and then run forward along the narrow walkway to reach another small platform which previously held a "?" marking a point of interest. With all three batteries in place, this area now holds a teleporter which takes you to another section of the ship, directly into a checkpoint.

# Ready for Action

Run to the edge of the platform where you see another object floating out a bit in midair. When you look down from the edge you can just see another of the trampoline platforms within jumping distance. Leap out onto it, then from the top of your jump, move forward to land on top of the device, using an extra jump in mid-air to really help target your fall.

It turns out that the device is actually a cannon, and as you land in its operation seat the huge number of entries in the wall around the room start to open, sending waves of drones after you! Start firing at them immediately by pressing your normal Attack button, using the crosshairs to direct your fire toward the nearest drones.

You need to withstand a pretty large wave of the drones before things are done. Constantly swivel your gun around to find and take out the closest threats—if you concentrate on the enemies at a safe distance in front of you, you might be missing the ones sneaking up very close from behind.

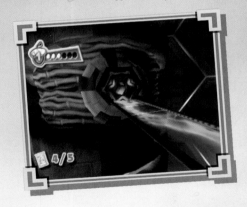

When their sensors turn red, that's when you especially have to worry, and make sure to take them out ASAP before they fire. Your cannon has a decent amount of health but it's not unlimited, so you don't want to let too many of the drones through. Check the radar at the top right of the screen for a handy guide to where the great numbers are at, and knock many out at once with a chain reaction, as a large number of the drones tend to explode when any one in a cluster blows up.

Once you blast away the final drone to appear, the door at the other side of the room opens and puts out a walkway between it and the original platform you landed on after your teleport. When the brief cut-scene showing this ends, you are automatically back on that original platform. Run across the walkway, but watch out for the lines of light along the path and jump over them, or lose an egg each time you touch one.

Once you reach the doorway run into the hall and through it, and you finally reach your destination, with another of the handy simulation devices nearby.

# Space Simulator II

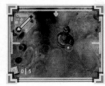

Unfortunately just making it through the ship isn't quite enough. The spacecraft's computer isn't through with our young friends just yet—it wants Chicken Little to pass another Space Simulator test before it lets the group do as it pleases. Guide Chicken Little through a second simulator to beat the computer, and give the friends free rein in the spaceship's control center.

## PS2

| | |
|---|---|
| ● | Shoot |
| ● (held down) | Shoot continuously while Rapid Fire Pickup is active. |
| △ | Missile (After Missile Pickup) |
| L1 | Tilt Left |
| R1 | Tilt Right |

## GC

| | |
|---|---|
| B | Shoot |
| B (held down) | Shoot continuously while Rapid Fire Pickup is active. |
| Y | Missile (while Missile Pickup is active) |
| L | Tilt Left |
| R | Tilt Right |

## XBOX

| | |
|---|---|
| X | Shoot |
| B (Held) | Continuously fire shots (while a Rapid Fire Pickup is active) |
| Y | Missile (while Missile Pickup is active) |
| L | Tilt Left |
| R | Tilt Right |

## ITEMS

**Health Pickup**
Restore some health to a damaged craft.

**Rapid Fire Pickup**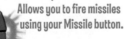
For a limited time allows you to hold down the Shoot button to continuously fire shots.

**Double Shot Pickup**
Fire paired energy blasts with each shot for a limited time.

**Missile Pickup**
Allows you to fire missiles using your Missile button.

**Shield Pickup**
Gives you extra shielding for a short period of time.

## DANGERS

Don't collide with the different objects and buildings floating by.

Avoid enemy fire, as well as the enemy ships.

## Second Mission

While in general this second mission is like the first, this time your view is from the top down. You can also move your craft forward and back on the screen using the directional pad or left analog stick, although the scenery keeps moving forward continuously no matter where you move on the screen.

The mission starts off somewhat slowly, with a tower off to the right holding a missile pickup, followed by a mine in the center of the screen, a few small enemy craft to the left then to the right, and another tower to the left. Between some of the enemy ships and the towers you should be able to get a rapid fire pickup quite early on, which lasts a short while. After the tower watch out for another mine toward the right just before you start to reach a field of asteroids, and the start of some open space.

After you make it past the first land mass and into the asteroids blast your way through, picking up the health pickups that show up occasionally when the asteroids are destroyed. Keep toward the right side of the screen, as the first **card** floats into view partway through the asteroid field.

Now you float back over a second land mass, with enemies picking up their pace and moving in to shoot at your craft. A rapid fire pickup really helps here, as you need to take out a whole string of enemies as quickly as possible. Very shortly after the smaller enemy ships appear you must start to dodge a stream of fire from a large craft that appears to the top right of the screen. Slip past the stream of fire to the right if it's at all possible, to set yourself up to fire upon the ship in return. Missiles are especially useful in taking out these larger craft.

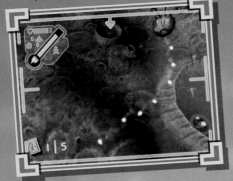

As you fly through a brief bit of open space destroy a mine in the center, then hug the right side of the screen to pick up another **card**. Move back in toward the center to assault a few towers as you fly by, followed by more streams of the fast red enemy craft. A short distance more, and chains of other orange ships fly out from both sides of the screen to try to catch you unaware. Hug the back of the screen and keep up as continuous a stream of fire as possible, doing your best to avoid the enemy's own fire in return. Don't relax even if you get rid of most of them, as more streams soon appear to back up the first. Also watch for a point where the enemy ships stream in around a cluster of towers in front of you, at the edge of more open space—behind the center tower is a **card** that you might not see, so take the tower out of your path and fly forward to get the prize.

As you float away from the second land mass and back into open space, stay toward the center of the screen to pick up another **card** very slightly to the left. From the start watch out for a mine as well as a string of red craft that appear and fire upon you, moving back and forth in a snake-like fashion. A steady stream of fire is the best way to take them out. These continue until you approach the next bit of land, with another mine waiting for you at the edge.

After three waves of the orange ships, the next enemies to appear are the small circular craft. There are a large number of these, and they take up odd formations to make it hard to predict their movement, so do your best to avoid their fire and strafe them as much as possible before they get too close. Once they're gone, be ready to fire upon another asteroid field in order to make it through in relatively one piece.

Strafe back and forth quickly to take out all of the next enemies, both the quick red ships that continue to attack at the edge of landfall, and the swarm of smaller craft that follows after them. You don't get much chance to breathe after taking these enemies out—another of the large green ships appears from the left and starts to fire upon you. Take it out quickly if you can, as chains of other smaller orange ships soon appear from the right then left to add to the assault. Luckily even if you don't take all of these orange ships out they leave the screen again soon, snaking down and back up as they cross their way to the other side, and out of view.

While taking out asteroids drift toward the left, where another large craft appears. Once again you shouldn't be too long in taking it out, as after only a brief pause a second large craft appears from the front right, and you want to be ready to slide past its fire on the right to be in line to return fire yourself.

As if you didn't have enough on your hands, watch as the land mass comes to an end to pick up a last **card** toward the left of the screen. Just after the card, you cross the white and black checkered strip that marks the end of your test, and a completed objective.

# Tube Surf

Once all three of the active friends are in the control room and Chicken Little has aced his latest test, the group can finally go about freeing Fish from his predicament. The fourth member of the group seems to be trapped in a holding tank, but the unhelpful aliens haven't labeled the controls to free him! While trying to get Fish out of hot water, the friends end up dropping him straight out of the tank, and into the frying pan. Guide Fish through the various tubes as he falls through them, until he can get back to safety inside the ship.

## PS2

 Jump
Shoot

## GC

 Jump
Shoot

## XBOX

Jump
Shoot

## DANGERS

Avoid any of the energy barriers stretched along your path.

Don't slip off any of the slides into open space, or you have to start over at your last checkpoint.

Watch out for small enemy drones in the shape of a ball. Shoot them down, before they get you.

Avoid the blades of the spinning fans in some tubes.

## Tube Ride

Your controls in this mad slide are limited—you can move Fish on his platform from side to side using the directional pad and left analog stick, you can jump using the Jump button, or you can shoot a few occasional bad guys out of the way using the Attack button. Your job this time isn't to find a path to safety, fight a lot of enemies or solve puzzles—instead you just need to do your best to keep Fish in the tubes and on the slides and keep him from smashing into things in the process.

Although you start out in a good solid tube, trouble isn't long in finding you. Energy barriers soon start to appear in your path. The first one sails by overhead if you haven't moved along the walls of the tube, but you need to swing to one side or the other to avoid the second. Swing out of the way twice more, as two more barriers appear each perpendicular to the last.

When you pass the fourth barrier watch for the upcoming end of the tunnel. The tube changes into a slide the size of only one side of the tube, so you need to make sure you're on the side of the tube that joins up with the slide to keep from flying out into open space. If this happens you go back to start, or at later spots just back to your last checkpoint. Checkpoints in this slide aren't marked by the normal checks—instead you hear a small tune play when you've passed one of the checkpoints.

Hang toward the right side of the slide, as very shortly it shifts over a bit, cutting off the left side but adding more space to the right. Move to the right again, as the slide repeats this shift after only a few seconds. One long curve later and the slide shifts back to the left, so be ready for it. It then goes right two more times before bringing you back into another full tunnel.

This time the central wire is joined by two more, one to each side. The right-hand wire holds a long string of acorns, while the left holds a **card** at its very end. It's best to pick up the card your first time through, then on any further trips you must make through this section, flip over to the right wire to pick up the acorns. To move between the wires, jump while moving in the direction of the next wire. The two side wires end before the center one meets up with the next tube, so make sure you jump back to safety before it's too late.

This time you have a whole series of energy barriers at closer intervals, so to avoid them you need to go into a controlled spin fully around the tube, to be constantly moving into the safe zones beside the barriers. Spin toward the left side, to best put yourself into position after the barriers—the tunnel ends and there is only a thin stream of energy to ride on, and to catch it you must be riding over a series of arrows as the tunnel comes to an end.

Walkthrough

The next section of tube holds more energy barriers, but this time they move back and forth between the sides of the tube. It's hard to judge their motion on the fly—do your best to slide past one side as the barrier is moving away, and make sure you bring your hex panel back around full circle by the end to be ready to hit the next section of slide on target.

As you head out on the wire of energy, press Attack to shoot down an enemy drone in front of you. Ride straight ahead through a very brief tube and onto the next slide. This one shifts right, and then right again, followed by two rapid left shifts, at which point another enemy appears in front of you. Shoot it down as you make one more shift to the left, then one to the right, and one last move to the left before the next tube.

Just after hitting the next slide it shifts twice to the left, then back to the right twice, and another two times to the left all in rapid succession. After sliding over a "hill" it again shifts to the right, and then left. At this point the slide surrounds you to form almost another tube, but immediately after the entire "floor" that made up the slide you came in on drops away, so as soon as it switches to the "tube" flip around along the right to reach the "ceiling" of the slide.

Once you flip around be ready to slide right again very shortly, then the slide joins back up with an actual tube. More energy barriers stretch across this section, but they don't move, so go into a controlled spin to avoid them. Be ready for another enemy to appear afterward, and shoot it down while watching for the next slide to appear, keeping yourself ready to meet it. Just as you enter the next slide, another **card** appears in the center, difficult to see.

Inside this tube you find a series of three spinning fans. You need to watch carefully to judge their motion, then slide through between the blades. After the third fan watch for the next arrows, pointing to your position to get onto the next energy wire.

After entering the next slide be ready to quickly shift left, then slide all the way left around to the other side of a "tube" that forms, before the slide drops away again. There are four more normal shifts to the left in a row before you enter the next bit of tube. Here you must slide past three more fans before coming back out onto the slide.

53

The slide shifts right and left quickly, then watch for the next strip of arrows pointing to an energy wire. This time another wire shortly appears to the right but your original wire drops away just after, so jump over to the next wire as soon as you can. Soon another wire appears to the left—jump to it before your current one also disappears, picking up a new **card** toward the start of the new slide if you're quick enough. This third wire goes directly into the next portion of the slide.

The first shift this time is far to the right, followed by two more similar shifts before you enter a tube. Here more of the bars of energy show up, but this time there are two at a time, moving back and forth. It's even more difficult now to try to judge an open space before you slide into it, so watch very carefully and slide toward the area from which both bars are currently moving away.

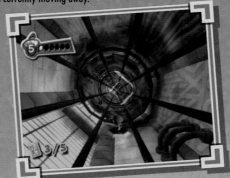

After four of the sets of barriers, more arrows appear at the end of the tube and you catch your next wire. This time you have to jump left and right in quick succession. You enter a tube with another enemy, but only ride it briefly before the next arrows point toward yet another wire. Again you must jump right, then left, as different wires appear and vanish.

The next section is much like a repeat of the last—three of the paired energy bars to slide through, then the arrows marking another wire. This time when a wire appears to the left the original doesn't end right away, but it does vanish eventually, so make the jump over as soon as you can. Now ride the second wire as far to the end as you can to grab a fourth **card** at the far end, and quickly jump over to the right again at the last second. Hop left again as soon as you can at the next wire, and again follow this left-hand wire to the end for the last **card**.

After you make the last-minute jump back to the right, the wire meets back up with a tube holding two more fans to slide around. Make sure you meet the next bit of slide at the end of the tube, and this takes you straight to the light at the end of the tunnel, and the end of the chapter.

# Cornfield Escape

The friends are back together again, but they don't have much time to celebrate. The aliens are back as well, and they don't look too happy to have the uninvited guests. The friends make it out of the ship in one piece, but that's just the start of their escape. Guide Chicken Little as he helps get all three of his friends through the cornfield near where the spacecraft landed, and then warns the town of the impending invasion!

## ITEMS

**Coin** Once you reach the farmyard., collect 15 of these to purchase a soda. The number of coins needed varies on difficulty.

## PS2

Jump
Double Jump
Yo-yo Attack
Pole Climb
Yo-yo Swing
(Held) Powershot
Grapple

## GC

Jump
Double Jump
Yo-yo Attack
Pole Climb
Yo-yo Swing
(Held) Powershot
Grapple

## XBOX

Jump
Double Jump
Yo-yo Attack
Pole Climb
Yo-yo Swing
(held) Powershot
Grapple

# DANGERS

Stay out of the searchlights, or you get zapped!

Watch out for the drones and robots, and destroy them before they hurt you.

Falling from too high up in the farmyard takes away an egg.

Don't go too far down into the well in the barnyard.

If you're walking the wires above the farmyard, jump over any electrical sparks.

During your final flight to the bell tower, dodge the UFOs that try to block your path.

Once you've gotten rid of the drone, run up to Runt. As soon as you touch him, you get his attention with a whistle, and he starts to follow you. Weave back between the searchlights. Don't worry about them touching Runt, just Chicken Little. Go into the dugout, which acts as a checkpoint. Runt stays here, and if you lose all your eggs after this point, he remains in the dugout. Now you just have two more friends to collect.

Fish-Out-of-Water is standing in the same direction you found Runt, but farther out. The biggest dangers are the drones near him and the two searchlights in front of him that sweep out and then back together. A good place to snipe at the patrol drones is the edge of a white spot out on the field, closest to Fish. This keeps you out of the lights' path and just close enough to hit a drone with a good shot, and the drone won't spot you. When it's gone, run between the spotlights while they're moving apart, and bring Fish back to the dugout the same way you brought Runt.

Now you just have Abby left to retrieve. She's off to the left once you leave the dugout, on the pitcher's mound between three spotlights. Watch for all three spotlights to move in at the same time and then back out. Then sneak in to tag Abby. Work your way back to the dugout with the last of your three friends, and your group makes its escape from the dugout into the nearby countryside.

# Catcher in the Corn

Just outside the ballpark, you must first make your way past a stream. Go straight ahead from your starting point, avoiding the first searchlight and destroying the patrol drone ahead. There's a right-hand path with a drone that you can sneak up behind and destroy, which puts you in a position to harass the drones across the river. Just be careful of a tricky spotlight here.

Once you're beside the riverbank, double jump to a rock in the water when the next searchlight is moving away. Pick up a **card**, and then jump onto the other bank. Pick off the drones hovering on this side, if you didn't destroy them from the other bank. Now wait for the pair of searchlights that were covering the left-hand drone to move away from each other, and run past. There's one more set of searchlights to watch out for beyond the first pair, and then you have a free run to the nearby farmyard.

You find yourself at the start of a cornfield, and you need to find your scattered friends once again. Take a few steps forward to pick off another drone with your slingshot. Then run forward into an open clearing that again acts as a checkpoint, just like the dugout. You need to find your friends in the cornfield and bring them back to this clearing for safety.

Right now, the only option is to run straight ahead from your starting point in the center of the maze. Stop where a dead end runs off to the left, and shoot the drone ahead of you. Then continue forward and take one fork around a tall batch of corn, being careful of the robot lurking on each side. Both left and right paths join up again past the bit of corn in the center, but there's another path off to the left that leads to a clearing with another robot. Take this side path if you need more acorns and you're confident about fighting. If not, go straight.

If you take the left into the clearing, wait for the robot to use its electric attack. Then run in to attack it with your yo-yo. The slingshot spins a robot around to stun it, which is useful here but does no actual damage. When the robot is gone, you have a whole clearing full of acorns to collect.

From the side clearing, return to the circle around the corn. Continue around it to reach another opening in the maze that leads to Runt, along with a robot. Take it out, and run up to Runt to have him follow you again.

Now it gets a bit trickier. When you pick up a friend, the searchlights are activated while you're heading back to the center of the maze. There are two lights that circle just around the cornstalks outside Runt's starting point. Run up next to the corn in the circle's center, and move between the searchlights. Make a break toward the other side when it's clear. Watch out for the robot on the side you haven't cleared already! Run right up alongside the wall as it dips outward, avoiding the next searchlight moving in small circles, and then watch out for searchlight that moves into and out of the dead end. Make a break for the center of the maze when you can, and concentrate on your other two friends.

Once you've rescued Runt, a new path opens up to the left of where you originally entered the clearing—to the right of where you're facing if you just ran in with Runt. Run forward along this new path until you reach another circle, and run around it on the right to find a path leading off to this side. Here you find another of the robots and some acorns, as well as the third **card** for you to collect.

Run back out and continue around the circle, taking the exit opposite the center of the maze. Stop just inside this exit to pick off the next drone, and then continue forward carefully. Just a bit farther in, you find a clearing with two more robots. Once they've shot at you, run in to take them down. Run back out if necessary, to avoid the second one's electric attack if you can't take down the first one in time. You can use your slingshot from a distance to stun them both.

Once both robots are out of the way, go back into the clearing to rescue Abby. Have her follow you toward the center of the maze, avoiding the searchlights. Watch out for a group of three robots that move in and then away. Time your move carefully. More searchlights prowl around the circle on this side and just around the exit into the maze's center, so stay on your toes.

With your second friend safe, another exit opens from the center of the maze, opposite where you're just entering the clearing with Abby. Run straight ahead through it, and stop at the edge of the first large clearing to pick off two drones. Run through the exit at the right side of the clearing to pick up some acorns. Now return and continue through the clearing, but be careful on the other side. Just after the exit from the clearing, you run across another robot. Be ready to face it down.

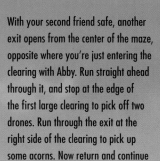

Go past the robot to reach a garbage can, and then turn left and follow the path. Be ready for another robot after a few turns, and another one hidden just behind the next corner. Expect another such guard at every intersection or corner, until you reach the clearing with Fish.

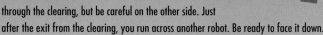

With your third friend behind you, retrace your path back through the maze. Be careful of the searchlights. Wait for them to start climbing the walls of corn away from the path, and then move past. Be careful of one on the ground by the trash can, slipping around as soon as it's safe. Watch out for another trio of lights to appear in the last big clearing before you rejoin your other friends. When the lights start to move out away from the center, slip around and through them to the other side of the clearing. One more light appears unexpectedly from the dead ends just beside the center of the maze, so don't run right into it. Let it pass.

When you lead Fish back into the central clearing, your group is ready to make its escape. Now you start to plan just how to warn the town of the impending alien attack. As your group moves into the farmyard, Chicken Little spots a soda machine, which gives him an idea.

Now cross over to the higher level on the opposite end of the barn. You can do this by jumping out and swinging over from where you collected the coin. Or you can return to where you grappled over to the hay and jump onto a beam running along the side of the barn, following it over to the other side. Once you're on the far end of the rafters, destroy the glowing crates in one corner with a Powershot to pick up another **coin**.

# Coin Collection

Now you must collect 15 coins to buy a soda, out of the 20 coins (number of coins varies with difficulty) scattered all around the farmyard. Your best bet is to collect all of the coins inside the barn first. This is a safe area and you can take your time. From there, take the coins you can get to the quickest and easiest with your own particular skills.

If you're facing the barn, away from the entrance, run forward and to the right to a blue-glowing stack of tires. Use a Powershot to break up these tires and collect your first **coin**, and then go to the left and jump onto the hay bales in the corner. From there, climb onto the pitchfork handle as if it were a pole. From the top of the climb, jump onto a ledge to pick up another **coin**.

Still on the same end of the barn, jump up onto the hay bales in the middle of the rafters. Standing in the very center, face toward the barn entrance and jump out to latch onto a pole with your yo-yo. As you swing out, let go. If you get it just right, you should collect a **coin** on your way out. Quickly latch onto the next pole, and on your next release, you should be able to adjust your landing and collect a **card** from midair. If you miss any of your swings but don't move to the right or left, you land on a beam running down the center of the barn. You can also use this beam to cross from one side to the other, but it's hard to climb onto it from the entrance side without falling.

Now run to the right side of the barn (if you're facing toward the back) and climb onto the bales of hay along that side, all the way to the top. Facing the wall with the entrance, use your grapple to latch onto a hook and pull yourself over to the top of a higher stack of hay. Jump onto a ledge, run across, and leap down to the next stack of hay to collect another **coin**.

When you're done collecting everything inside the barn, go up to the rafters on the side of the barn opposite the door. Here you find a window. Climb outside, and there's a ledge here to support you. Follow this ledge to the right, and double jump onto another small platform. Turn the corner to follow a rain gutter along the outside of the barn, until you reach a place where various shingles are sticking out.

Use these shingles as footholds, and jump up to another ledge outside a window. Pick up the **coin** here. From this ledge, continue along the gutter to the top of some hay bales, and then climb the stack of hay up toward the front wall of the barn. Use it to jump onto a ledge around the corner. Pick up the **coin** on this ledge, and then use the platform as the starting point of a trail with many more coins.

From the far end of the ledge, double jump onto a slanted board on the side of the silo. Immediately run up toward the opposite end, because the board starts to tilt right after you land on it. Quickly double jump over to the next board around the silo, and then run toward the end and double jump to a third board.

From the third board, run as far as you can before it starts to tilt very much, and jump out onto the nearby roof as far up as you can. If you fall from any of the boards, be careful, because one of the robots patrols near the silo. To get back up to the tilting boards, run to the right side of the barn (when facing it), climb onto the hay bales there, and start the trip again.

Once you're on the side of the roof, you may start to slide if you haven't jumped high enough. Sometimes you can keep jumping repeatedly to gain a bit of ground; other times you fall to the ground and have to return to the start and try again. Once you get to a certain point up the roof, you reach a few shingles you can use as a foothold, and then a spot where it's no longer slippery. Then you can run up it as normal.

On top of the roof, you find another **coin**. Now you have a choice to make. If you've collected all of the coins up to this point, you can skip the next section along the electric wires and collect all the other coins in the farmyard to get enough for a soda. While you're up here, you can also go forward and climb the pole at the end of the roof. This takes you to a section with five more coins, but it's a bit more dangerous.

If you do decide to go on from the top of the pole, slide down a wire to the top of the silo. Cross over to the window at the other side of the room. From the board in the window, run straight out along the wire. Don't move to the right or left, and watch out for blue electrical sparks that move toward you along the wire. Whenever a spark is about to reach you, keep moving forward as you jump over it.

When you reach the platform at the top of the telephone pole, jump over to the other platform just to the right for an acorn. Then leap up onto the portion of the pole holding the **coin**, and wait for the next electrical spark to come by before running out onto the next wire. As you reach the end of this wire, jump up to the top of the pole for the next **coin**. Be careful not to jump too far, or you might fly off the other side and down to the ground—very painfully.

From here, turn at an angle and run along the next wire. The next pole is the same as the one you just left, with a **coin** and the next wire on the opposite side. This time the electrical pulse is moving in the same direction as you, so step between pulses and run at the same pace as the sparks to keep from being shocked.

At the top of the next pole, pick up the **coin**. Then run along one more wire to where a pole holds a **coin** over the farmhouse roof. After you collect this last coin, jump down to the roof. From here you can collect the other coins along the rooftops (see toward the end of this subsection), or make your way down to the ground level to pick up coins around the farmyard.

Once you pick up any high-flying coins you want, start on the easier-to-reach coins outside the barn. Straight out from the entrance is a well. Be careful approaching it, because there are two robots that may wander around nearby. Fight them off if necessary. Then jump onto the edge of the well, jump toward the center of the well, and quickly press the Attack button to latch on with your yo-yo, just as if you were climbing a pipe. Pick up the **coin** inside the well, but don't climb too far down or you lose an egg. As soon as you get the coin, climb back out onto safe ground.

From the bales of hay, jump to the roof of the house. Run along the flat part to where the roof links up with a higher roof. Climb up one side of that roof and down the other to reach the last **card**. Climb back up to the top of the roof, run to the opposite end, and double jump onto a lower roof in front of the barn to collect another **coin**.

Before you jump down, run back along the top of the new roof toward the farmhouse. Double jump from the roof over to a stack of crates to collect the **coin**. From here, jump back down to the ground to collect any other coins you've missed so far.

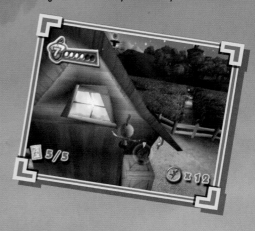

Now for the left side of the barn, as you face it from the outside. Just beside the silo in the corner of the yard is another stack of tires. Destroy them with a Powershot, and the **coin** inside is yours for the taking. There's another coin on the right side of the barn. In this corner you find a stack of crates. Climb them and destroy the top crate using a Powershot to get the **coin** inside.

If you didn't pick up the coins high up along the outside of the barn, or you fell while trying to climb along the outside of the silo to pick up the coins along the electrical wires, the hay bales along this side of the barn also lead up to that trail.

Once you've picked up at least 15 coins (number of coins varies with difficulty), go to the vending machine next to the farmhouse and step into the ? icon. Just as he did back at the school, Chicken Little shakes up the pop and uses it as a rocket to blast off.

When you're done around the barn, check the left side of the farmhouse when facing it. Here you find another stack of tires tucked away in the corner. Powershot them to get the **coin** inside. Now continue behind the house, and climb the bales of hay to reach another **coin** at the top.

Watch out for the UFOs that turn sideways, their dangerous blades ready to stop your flight. Dodge around them, and fly straight at the bell in the school's bell tower. This warns the town and successfully ends the chapter.

# Cannon Chaos

Chicken Little and his friends have warned the town of the alien invasion, and now the streets are full of panic as the aliens start to descend. It's up to you to help the mayor, Turkey Lurkey, use the town's trusty cannon to keep the citizens safe!

## PS2

| | | |
|---|---|---|
| ⬜ | | Shoot |
| ⬜ | (Hold) | Super Shot |

## GC

| | | |
|---|---|---|
| ⚫ | | Shoot |
| ⚫ | (Hold) | Super Shot |

## XBOX

| | | |
|---|---|---|
| ⚫ | | Shoot |
| ⚫ | (Hold) | Super Shot |

## DANGERS

Don't let any blasts from enemy spaceships get through your defenses.

## Turkey Shoot

The idea behind this chapter is simple, although the execution can be a bit hard. The enemy spaceships attack in three waves, and you need to knock them all of out of the fight without getting shot in return. After the first wave, the top-right corner of the screen has a display of how many ships you still have to shoot down. Once those ships are down, that wave ends and the next begins.

For the first wave, you have no counter and the normal life bar is grayed out. This is because there are only a handful of flying saucers to shoot down, and all of them are on the screen. They're not paying attention to Turkey Lurkey or his cannon at the moment. You just need to fire on each one until it takes enough damage to send it flying back up into the sky, away from your barrage. Each one takes a few normal shots before running away, although a super shot speeds up the process. If you have to swing your gun around to aim, hold the button down to charge up the shot while you're aiming.

Once the first wave is gone, another wave descends. This time you have a total of 12 ships to take out. Now that you've shot at the enemy, they're not going to leave you alone. These ships fire off balls of energy that damage you and take away an egg if they connect. You can stop these enemy shots by shooting them, so switch between firing on the enemy ships and firing at their energy blasts. If an enemy fires at you from offscreen, a red arrow shows you the direction it's coming from. If you lose all your eggs, you must start the wave over again.

Not all 12 enemy ships are onscreen at once. When you knock out a few, more come down. When you get down to the last few ships, things get easier because you don't have as many foes firing at you. Of course, getting that last ship in your sights long enough to take it out can be difficult, but be patient and you can do it.

The third wave brings a bit of a twist. You only have three ships to blast down, but this time their shields are tougher, and the cannon is moving around the town square on the back of a truck. This makes it a bit more difficult to aim, because the truck and the UFOs are moving in different directions and at different speeds. Concentrate more on keeping the enemy fire under control. Since these ships are shielded most of the time, you need to wait until just before or after an enemy fires to actually do some damage.

With the third wave gone, Turkey Lurkey has succeeded in fending off the invasion so far. But the *real* action is going on at your next stop.

# Firetruck Frenzy

While Turkey Lurkey is doing an admirable job defending the town square from invaders, Chicken Little and his dad are cutting off the invasion at its root. It appears that the cause of the trouble is a little alien child who's been separated from his parents somehow. Chicken Little has spotted him, and now he and his father need to get this cosmic kid back to the ship. This is where the friends come in, with a firetruck they've borrowed during the chaos. You need to drive the firetruck around town to keep up with the flying saucer, until you can catch the alien family's attention somehow.

## PS2

| | |
|---|---|
| ✕ | Accelerate |
| ☐ | Brake |
| △ | Reverse |
| L1 | Powerslide |
| R1 | Powerslide |

## GC

| | |
|---|---|
| A | Accelerate |
| X | Brake |
| Y | Reverse |
| L | Powerslide |
| R | Powerslide |

## XBOX

| | |
|---|---|
| A | Accelerate |
| B | Brake |
| Y | Reverse |
| L | Powerslide |
| R | Powerslide |

## ITEMS

**Energy Loop**

   Drive through these to add precious seconds to your clock.

## DANGERS

 If your timer runs out, you must start the mission over.

## Firefighter

You've been through the town in a vehicle before, but those errands were nothing like this. You start out with only 10 seconds on your clock at the top of the screen. If the timer runs out, you have to restart the chapter from the very beginning. The more times you fail the chapter, though, the longer the time you get to start with.

The key to this mission is that the alien spaceship lets out strange loops of energy as it travels through the town. Whenever you touch one of these energy loops, it adds 3.5 to your clock. So you have to blaze through town, hot on the trail of the UFO, and hit almost every energy loop along the way.

Because you're in such a rush and moving along some tight turns, the Powerslide comes in handy. Hitting one of the top shoulder buttons, while turning sharply, takes you into a slide. This can really help you get past some tight situations in no time flat. It's easy to overdo the turn and end up facing the entirely wrong direction, though, so be careful. If you're facing the wrong way and need to get back in control, you can use a sharp Powerslide or a sudden brake to turn yourself completely around.

Just after you've caught the first loop, the ship takes a sharp turn to the left near the courthouse. There's a **card** over by the courthouse steps. Since you've barely gotten started, you can just keep going straight, grab the card straight off, and make the sacrifice of starting over again. Otherwise, turn sharply left, with a Powerslide if you need it, to follow the ship.

The next turn is also a left, at the end of a fenced section and off the blacktopped road onto a lighter-colored road. Don't get carried away with the Powerslide here. The trail soon turns slightly right and then left a few more times, and you need to stay in control. The curves are a bit more gentle for the most part, but watch out when you see a stop sign toward the right.

After the next sharp right turn, look for a crater to your left, and a tree that crashes down right behind it. Avoid them both by hugging the right side of the road. After the next loop of energy, the same thing happens to the right. A few slight twists later, you need to make a very sharp right turn back onto the paved road.

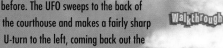

Just after you pass the sign, the ship knocks down a burning telephone pole on the left side of the road. Steer far over to the right to avoid it, and then watch out for the pavement that's been disturbed over to the right side of the road.

Next, the path twists a bit and runs in front of the courthouse, where you should grab the card by the steps if you didn't before. The UFO sweeps to the back of the courthouse and makes a fairly sharp U-turn to the left, coming back out the same direction it just came in. You can cut across the rear courthouse lawn to catch up to it a bit more, but you'll miss a few energy loops in the process.

When you see a farmhouse to your left, dodge right again to avoid another crater, and then left to avoid yet another. After a fairly steep turn to the left, watch for another stop sign on the right, with an abandoned vehicle on the left. Another crater is about to appear to the right, so get to the other side, or hug the road very far to the right. Then a telephone pole falls from the left, so you need to avoid that on the right side.

The UFO gradually winds back up a familiar road. Dodge two craters to each side, and then watch for a crashing telephone pole to the left. Dodge another crater on the right, and one to the left. Be careful not to crash into too many fences or hedges as the saucer flies back through more houses. After a left turn past a stop sign, watch for a crater to the right, followed by a car crashing to the left. This is followed by more craters to the left and right, so keep weaving between them. At this point, watch for a group of low

Once the pole falls, keep a close watch for a low fence that you can crash through to appear on the right. Another **card** is here, inside the corner of the fence, so aim for that corner of the yard as you pass through. You now have some tricky dodging to do between a crater, a wrecked car, and another crater as you follow the ship.

After the crater, you pass another tall fence that stretches to your right. Almost at the end of this fence, start turning to the left to crash through a hedge and low fence, and pick up another **card**. Watch out for some other vehicles on the next stretch of road, as well as a crater to the left.

As you leave the houses, watch for another telephone pole to crash down from the left and then the right, and then a tree to the left. Just to the right of the tree is a **card** for you to pick up as you drive by. Angle your firetruck carefully through the covered bridge after passing by the tree. Just after the bridge, the UFO starts to fly by the courthouse again, and the chapter comes to a screeching halt.

# Tube Tumble

Once the firetruck catches up to the spaceship, Chicken Little has to get the little guy back to his parents. He has to climb to the top of the courthouse to get their attention, but unfortunately, this catches the attention of other aliens too! At the last minute, the whole group is beamed up into the spaceship, but the guys are split up once again. To start with, help Runt get through the tubes of the spaceship while he's in a wild tumble.

## PS2
○ Jump

## GC
Ⓐ Jump

## XBOX
● Jump

## DANGERS

Don't touch the energy barriers along the tubes.

Jump over any red barricades set up along the tubes, or you start back at a checkpoint.

If you fall off the slides and into space, you start again at the last checkpoint.

Avoid any of the fire jets set up along the slides.

Avoid the blades of the fans along the tube.

## Runt in Space

This chapter is much like the earlier stage where you had to guide Fish through various tubes, except this time you don't shoot down any enemies. Just navigate Runt around the dangers in his way, and bring him through (relatively) safely.

The first danger is a series of three the energy barriers to tumble around. These are soon followed by a red barricade of sorts, jutting up from each side of the tube. Jump over this, or you get sent back to the start. Keep toward the side of the tunnel with the white line along it, so that when the tube turns into a half-pipe, you're on the solid part and not flying off into space.

Once you're in the slide, keep to the left to avoid a jet of fire that appears to the right. This is followed by one in the middle and another to the right, with one more to the left just before you go back into a tube.

At this point, you have another of the red barriers to jump. Then it's a series of four moving bars of energy to avoid. Do a controlled roll around the sides of the tube. Near the last energy bar is a **card**, so watch for it and get in position to grab it on your way past.

Just a bit farther down, you jump over another red barricade and then make your way between jets of fire. When the white line appears, take it as the "bottom" of the tube. Avoid the first two fire jets by rolling along one side of the tunnel, and then go back along the bottom to roll under the next three jets. Stay along the white line as you jump over one more red barricade. Then the tube becomes an even narrower slide than before.

As the slide starts to twist and turn, you may have to correct your course slightly to keep from rolling over one of the sides. Watch out for a jet of fire along the slide, and jump over it. After the fire, watch out for a ring holding another red barricade to jump through, followed by three more fire jets to jump over before the slide becomes a tube again.

At the start of the next tunnel, you make your way through three more energy barriers. They're moving in pairs, making it tough to slip through the empty areas. Next, jump through another red barrier, and quickly flip over to the "top" of the tube to avoid four jets of fire in a row taking up the bottom half. Flip back to the opposite side of the tube to avoid four new jets. Then jump through the next red barricade, picking up a **card** as you do so.

At the end of the tube is a series of three fans. Avoid the blades while you orient yourself back on the white line, before the tube becomes a half-pipe again. When you see another ring appear around the pipe, jump through the red barricade that appears, and then stay slightly left along the pipe to grab the next **card**. Quickly get down to the very center to roll under a pair of fire jets. Then roll to one side to avoid the next jet in the center of the slide, just before it becomes a tube again.

Now you have three more of the paired moving energy bars to avoid, followed by a barricade and three energy bars. As you go through the last of the bars, get back to the white line and be ready for the next slide to split into two. Move along the left side to grab a **card**, and be careful because it's very easy to slip off into space here.

As the two slides join back up, you enter the next tube. A whole series of non-moving energy bars jut out at different angles. Go into a controlled roll toward the left to slip past them and still be in the correct spot when the tube ends and a narrow slide begins along the white line.

Just after the slide begins, you must jump through another barricade. Then avoid fire jets to the right, left, right, and left again. Just after the last jet of fire, jump to grab a last **card**. Then roll into the next tube, and victory!

65

# Alien Little

With Runt more or less safe, it's Chicken Little's turn to navigate through the ship. He was beamed up into the ship with his father and the alien baby, but getting through the ship is his responsibility. He's facing dangers that are fairly familiar by now. Use every resource to get Chicken Little through the ship safely!

## PS2

 Jump

Double Jump

Slingshot (hold to aim, release to shoot)

(Near an alien walker) Enter alien walker

Yo-yo Attack

(held) Powershot

**Alien Walker Controls:**

Enter and Exit Walker

R Rotate top of Walker

L Move Alien Walker

R1 Fire Cannon

L1 Pick up Object

## GC

 A Jump

A A Double Jump

X Slingshot (hold to aim, release to shoot)

X (Near an alien walker) Enter alien walker

Yo-yo Attack

(held) Powershot

**Alien Walker Controls:**

Enter and Exit Walker

Rotate top of walker

Move Alien Walker

R Fire Cannon

L Pick up Object

## XBOX

 Jump

Double Jump

Slingshot (hold to aim, release to shoot)

(Near an alien walker) Enter alien walker

Yo-yo Attack

(held) Powershot

**Alien Walker Controls:**

Enter and Exit Walker

R Rotate top of walker

L Move Alien Walker

R Fire Cannon

L Pick up Object

## ITEMS

 Health Pickup

While in an alien walker, use this to restore some of its health.

## DANGERS

 Avoid being shot by the drones.

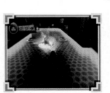 Don't trigger any more mines than you must, and quickly dodge the blasts of those you do set off.

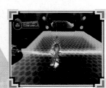 Don't step into the energy barriers!

 Stand away from the red crates once they're triggered and about to explode.

# Familiar Craft

This chapter should be somewhat familiar after you've navigated through the Alien Abby section. The layout and commands are quite similar in many places, and you need to use some of the same strategies. Other tactics are new to this level, though.

Run directly forward through the first doorway without falling off the platform. Through the door you find an alien walker, along with the first checkpoint. Climb into the walker, and blast the two switches beside the door with your laser beam to open the way to the next section.

In the next part of the hallway, you find drones to the right, left, and straight ahead when you enter. Strafe them with your laser, and move the boxes out of the way with your tractor beam if you need a clear shot. The switches for the next door are right beside the door. Trigger them when the drones are gone, and step through.

The next section has a number of drones down the hall. Snipe at them with your laser from back by the door. When you've cleared the path a bit, step toward an energy barrier across the path. To the right of the barrier, past the wall, are two generators that keep it running. Shoot the one from the sidelines. Then lift the red crate to the left with your tractor beam, swing it around, and toss it into the other generator's protective shield. Once they're gone, wait for the energy beam to flicker a bit and die down. Then quickly slip past the barrier and alongside the mine in the center of the hallway. Be careful, because the energy barriers on this level tend to flicker more after being deactivated than they did on the previous level. They can still deal some heavy damage to your craft.

On the opposite side of the barrier, there are more drones. There are a few around the corner, as well as more patrol drones coming out of two portals in the corner of the hall. While you shoot at the enemies, be careful of the red crate in the center of the hall. If you or the drones trigger it with your shots, make sure you stand back while it goes off.

Once the enemies are gone, you must once again use the red crate to smash two more shields protecting the switches off to the sides of the hall. As you've seen before, one shield is also protected by two pistons continuously moving together and apart, so time your throw carefully. If you're having difficulty with the timing, throw the crate just before it explodes.

When the next door slides open, be ready to start firing your laser. A good number of drones are ready to attack, including some farther off to the sides of the area. Toward the more open part of the room are multiple portals that bring in more drones. As you move forward, be ready to shoot them down as they appear, again being careful of the red crate in the center of the floor. If you're being attacked by a large number of drones and have a space to retreat to, fire at the crate to trigger it, and back up. It explodes and takes out some of your enemies for you.

After a few waves of the drones from the sides of the open area, they stop pouring out. When you destroy the last one, it opens the doors. Now use the red crate to knock out all the generators for each side of the room, shutting down the bar of energy across the floor. Once the flicker dies down for a moment, step past it into the next room, where you find a checkpoint. As soon as you trigger it, the next door slides open, with more enemies waiting on the other side.

Two portals are near the corner of this next hall, but only one of them eventually stops sending out more drones. The one straight ahead never stops. Once you've taken down all of the active drones and the side portal is quiet, slip over beside the still-active portal. At the next door, quickly trigger the switch to the right. Now you have one more switch over in the corner, protected by a shield, and you can't reach it alone.

Wait for the next drone to appear in the hall. Instead of shooting it with your laser, grab it. It cannot shoot while you're holding it, so carry it over to the shielded switch and launch it at the barrier, just as you would a red crate. Be careful while swinging it around. If you smash it against the wall while trying to get it in place, it's destroyed and you have to pick up the next one that appears. Once you've destroyed the shield with the drone, you can trigger the second switch, unlocking the door.

Go through into the next section, destroying one or two drones as they appear behind you. Once they're out of firing range, ignore any more that appear there for the moment. Instead, turn and concentrate on the drones in the hallway ahead of you. There's one red crate in this hallway, but once it's gone, it doesn't reappear. You need to destroy *two* generators to knock out the next two barriers of energy.

Go back to the previous section, grab one of the drones with your tractor beam, and carry it back to use it against the generator shields. If you destroyed the red crate by accident or didn't throw it well enough, repeat the process for the other generator. Once the generators are gone, be careful when going through the barriers. There are two, and you need to time your crossing between their flickering electricity. Then trigger the switches beside the door, if they weren't already triggered during the firefight.

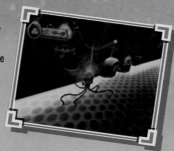

At the doorway, stop and fire at the drones in the section ahead. Once they're gone, you're faced with a whole field of mines. Pick up the red crate from the side of the hall and swing it over to the mines. Release the button to set the crate down between some of the crates, and back up. If you put it in a good spot, it takes some of the mines with it when it explodes. Do this as many times as needed to clear a path, and cross carefully over to the other side.

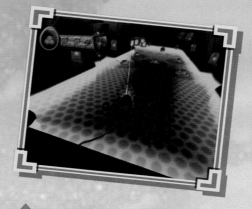

Watch out for the drones, both around the corner and appearing from the portals in the walls. Once you've taken out as many as you can, grab the one that reappears constantly, and throw it at the generator to the right side of the doorway. This generator is also guarded by four mechanisms that open and close at slightly different speeds, so time your throw very carefully. If you're having trouble with the timing, wait for the two sets of arms to start moving together. After you've triggered that switch, the second is just beside the door to the left.

Now you enter another large open area with four portals. If too many drones come out of the portals at once, shoot down the extras. Whenever you're left with just one, grab it with the tractor beam and throw it at one of the four generators around the room. Once the shields are gone and you've destroyed the generators, the two nearest energy beams break down. Now you have to navigate the beams carefully to grab a patrol drone on the other side. Use it to break down the last four generators, taking down the last energy barriers in front of the door. Watch out behind you as well. Make sure none of the drones appearing in the first section are within range to fire at you from behind.

Past the doorway, you find a landing pad. Use it to exit the walker, and jump through the person-sized doorway. Step onto the rising platform in the center of the next room, and ride it up. Just a slight way up, you're prompted to save your game, ending the chapter.

# Gravity Grab

Chicken Little has used the aliens' own technology against them in getting through the ship so far, but now he has to rely on his own two feet. Help him fight his way through the last sections of the spacecraft, using nearly every ability he has along the way. He needs to collect 20 coins (number of coins varies with difficulty) before he's done, to break through the barrier into the last part of the ship. Don't give up now—you're almost there!

Walkthrough

## PS2

- Jump
- Double Jump
- Slingshot (Hold to aim, release to fire)
- Yo-yo Attack
- Pole Climb
- Yo-yo Swing
- Grapple

## GC

- Jump
- Double Jump
- Slingshot (Hold to aim, release to fire)
- Yo-yo Attack
- Pole Climb
- Yo-yo Swing
- Grapple

## XBOX

- Jump
- Double Jump
- Slingshot (Hold to aim, release to fire)
- Yo-yo Attack
- Pole Climb
- Yo-yo Swing
- Grapple

## ITEMS

**Battery**

Pick up two of these and put them in place to power the teleporter.

**Coin**

Collect 20 to get past the final barrier!

## DANGERS

Don't touch the laser beams guarding some of the hallways.

Watch out for the robots' electric attacks!

Don't break open the glowing violet globes or you may be damaged by flying glass.

Don't fall when navigating high-up spaces!

Get off the smaller platforms before they turn red.

Watch out for any energy barriers you come across.

Don't leap through the red "shield" surrounded some platforms, or you hurt yourself.

Jump over the pulses of energy moving along the wires you walk.

Don't let the drones shoot you down.

Leap over the lines of energy along the final walkway.

# Zero Gravity

This level is in many ways like the "Space Alarm" section, but this time even more dangerous, so watch your step! Although the idea of the chapter is to collect enough coins to break through the final barrier, they're all found together at the end of the level, so don't worry about watching for them (or for the five cards) just yet.

Run through the first door, but be careful of the three laser beams in one portal moving back and forth, and time your approach for when they're generally moving away, leaving you an empty space to slip through. Inside the first room you find a checkpoint, but also one of the familiar robots. Approach quickly, and take it out with your yo-yo before it has a chance to attack you.

By now you should have an idea what happens next. More of the robots start to appear, the first from the front right room. With it gone, the next appears from the rear left. Destroy each in turn to turn the room back to normal and move on.

Once the enemies are gone and the room goes back to normal, take the acorns from the glass globes in each room. This time the next door opens automatically when the robots are gone, so once you have the acorns run through to the next checkpoint.

If the robots seemed familiar, this next bit should as well. You must jump across a chain of transparent platforms floating down. Now there is less time to delay than before—if you are too slow getting across, your last platform may be too low for you to jump onto the solid ground in the center of the room.

Once you do manage to get across in a short enough time, turn to the left and use your slingshot on the switch above a yellow-framed door. Stand close to the edge of the platform for this, as when the timed platforms appear there is very little time for you to start jumping across in order to make it, since this timer has been shortened as well.

## The Next Cycle

Another room, another checkpoint, and another group of guards to destroy. When the original is gone, the next two appear from the back left, then the back right. One more appears from the front right before you're done.

Once again collect the acorns; there are a few in the rooms with the switches as well. When you are done stand in the center of the room and trigger one of the two switches with your slingshot. Since this is another case where the timer is shorter than before, start to swivel your slingshot around the room even before your first shot hits, then as soon as you home in on the next switch, let fly another shot. When you get both switches under the time limit, a platform carries you up to the next level.

When your platform reaches the ledge encircling the room, jump to it and run in through the doorway to the next checkpoint. Trigger the switch dead ahead for the next set of platforms, and jump quickly along them to reach the center. This time your target is the switch over an orange-framed doorway, around your current height. Another set of (short) timed platforms appears, so make your way across to the next checkpoint, and coincidentally the next set of guards.

Now after the first robot is gone, one appears from the front left, with the next coming from straight ahead. The next comes from the rear right, with one last guard appearing from the rear left at the same time another comes from the front right. Be on hand to

knock one of these out immediately, then avoid the second's electric attack until you can move in to take it out as well. Once both of these final foes are down, the room becomes normal again. This time you have three timed switches to hit, all around the room, so waste no time between triggering them.

In the next room after landing on the ledge trigger the switch for the platforms again, and when you reach the center, the next door is a red-rimmed portal a bit below your current level. Hit the switch, and race across the timed platforms this time heading gradually down. Enter the hallway beyond the door, and watch for the three lasers guarding the point halfway through. Through the next door you reach another checkpoint, and a bit of a change from the rest of the level so far.

There are six trampolines along this next chain, so gauge each jump carefully to reach the next in line, especially as they curve slightly around to the left as they get higher. The last trampoline holds another checkpoint. Jump in place here for a while and watch your next target. Two small platforms rotate around a larger, solid platform. You need to time your jump from the trampoline to land on one of those platforms to ride. Get an extra "kick" with a second jump in midair if you need it to zero in on the platform.

# Change of Pace

Now you face more of the platforms that flicker red, at which point they damage you if you're standing on them. The first chain is three of these platforms in a row. Wait for the first one to go to solid blue and start jumping across quickly, as there isn't much time to spare. Jump to each platform as it turns blue, and from the last of the three perform a single jump and latch onto a nearby glass object with your yo-yo, starting to swing. Let go at the furthest point of your swing, then press Attack to latch onto the next.

Time your second swing carefully, because your next target is another of the red-flickering platforms and you need to release your hold to reach it as the red light has just died down. Waste no time in jumping along two more of the same platforms, and again along two more swings afterward. When you release from the second swing you fly this time onto a trampoline, and a handy checkpoint.

Once you're on your moving target, watch for the first energy barrier coming up. In the previous section you would jump to the solid platform before reaching the bar of energy, but this time the center platform is mostly surrounded by a red shield of energy that damages you if you try to jump into it, so you're stuck riding around the platform for a bit. When you approach the bar of energy jump and move forward slightly—make sure you're far enough back on your platform at the start of the jump that this doesn't send you off into space.

Repeat this two more times, then a clear space in the red shield surrounding the platform appears, so jump through it onto the solid structure. Now ride the moving platform from this solid area up into the air, and jump off when you get to the larger platform at the top of the structure (ignoring the smaller platform just underneath it). Make sure you trigger the checkpoint before moving on.

71

Just over by the checkpoint is a wire connecting this tower and another. Electrical pulses move constantly along this wire, so wait for one to pass and then step out onto the line. Run straight across, jumping over every pulse, and land on the other tower where you should trigger the next checkpoint.

Now next to this checkpoint look carefully over the edge and you see more trampolines stretching out into the distance. Jump down to the first, and then over to the next in line. On this second trampoline you must once again jump in place until you reach high enough to latch onto an object to swing from. Once you manage to grab it with your yo-yo, go straight forward from the swing to land on another trampoline with a checkpoint.

From this third trampoline you again have to latch onto a swing, this time swinging through upright metal poles onto the next trampoline. From here you have a chain of two more. Carefully jump onto the next red platform when it's safe, from there to another trampoline with yet another checkpoint, and along a chain of three more red platforms to another swing.

From this anchor, swing out and latch onto a second, and from there swing onto another trampoline through another set of the metal poles. From the first trampoline you reach a second with a checkpoint, and now you need to jump onto another of the moving platforms around a larger solid base. Once on the moving platform jump over one bar of energy, then quickly jump into an open space on the solid platform to avoid a larger field of energy that the moving plate goes directly through. Run along the clear space to the other side of the energy field and jump back onto the platform (or a later one), jump two more energy bars, and then leap into the larger clear space on the solid platform.

Here as before, ride one of the rising platforms to the top of the tower, and run across the electrified wire. From the next tower you jump onto a chain of three trampolines, leading to a large solid platform with a checkpoint. Now you should see another familiar sight—three devices, one of which has a battery in it already, and in the distance a point of interest marking a teleportation pad.

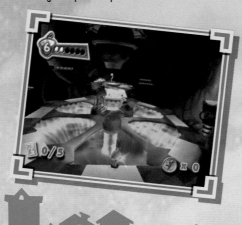

Turn toward the left, hit the switch floating off in the distance, and run along the clear platforms that appear without delaying. From the second set of platforms, jump down to a trampoline and over to the next set. When you reach the end of the blue-tinted platforms look to the right and hit another switch to bring up a set of yellow platforms leading further. The yellow platforms start at your current location, but don't delay in hitting the switch as you're still on the timer.

Run along the first couple yellow platforms, jump up to swing from one object, and swing across onto the next platforms. At the end of the chain jump off onto a more solid platform holding the second **battery**. Wait for the timer to run down, and hit the switch that you can reach from this platform. Now another set of blue platforms appears. Jump along the chain of trampolines, then across the rest of the blue platforms, and from there quickly to the central platform, where brushing against one of the devices puts the battery in place.

Now go to the other side of the platform and hit this switch, again wasting no time in jumping along the clear blue platforms. Watch the next solid platform you land on, as it is one of the red-lit platforms that can damage you at the wrong time. A few more platforms, and you reach another solid platform—this one looks like those that light up, but it's safe. Swivel here and hit the switch to the right, to bring up more of the yellow platforms.

Jump along the yellow platforms to reach three more solid but dangerous red platforms, then more of the yellow, which in turn take you to the last **battery**. Once again another switch brings up more of the light blue platforms, and from there you reach a trampoline. Jump up and immediately latch onto a swing from this trampoline, as you have no time at all to waste. Swing out, latch onto a second swing, and from there swing onto another of the blue platforms, jumping across to the solid central platform with no time to spare.

Once the third battery is in place, run forward to take the teleport to yet another familiar space. Jump from this next platform to a trampoline behind you, and from there into the seat of an energy cannon. Blast the waves of drones as they come out of the walls toward you, not letting them get close enough to let off a shot if you can help it.

First jump high into the air toward the right to pick up a coin from in the air, and land over on the lower platform on the right to grab the first **card**. From here jump up and out to pick up two coins from midair, and land on the platform below. Turn back toward the entrance and jump, and use a bit of debris as a launch pad to collect another **card** and a coin after it.

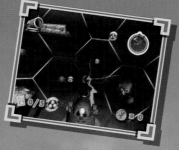

When the drones are gone and you find yourself back on the central platform run forward along the walkway, jumping over the moving red lines of energy below your feet. Run through the hallway (and last batch of lasers), and into a strange room that this time is different from one you've seen before.

Make your way back up to the original platform, and this time jump up and to the left to retrieve another **card**. Just out from this platform are two more coins in midair. There is another coin beside the tree, land on the tree to get it.

# Falling

This one last room holds all of the coins and all of the cards that you can collect on this stage. It looks initially like you won't be able to get to them at all—all of the platforms are very far apart, and even the bits of debris floating around the room are spaced farther than you should be able to reach with a jump.

Now jump freely between the various debris and platforms, collecting remaining coins all floating freely in the air. For the remaining cards, collect the fourth by starting on the final platform in front of the door, and jumping up and left to a platform and the **card**. A couple of the harder-to find coins are up here as well. Another semi-hidden coin is tucked away behind the tree floating to the right of the exit—the last **card** is also near here, in mid-air between the tree and exit.

The trick here is that this room has less gravity than the Earth, or even the rest of the ship. So while the center platform for example looks much too far away, you can reach it in one jump here, while a double-jump would take you even further.

Once you've collected at least fifteen (number varies with difficulty), jump across to the point of interest marking the exit. Touch the large "?" mark, and run through the now-open door into the next room, where you may save your progress.

# Space Simulator III

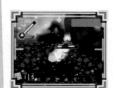

Now that Chicken Little has made his way back through the ship, he must convince the computer once more that he's a skilled enough pilot to have his own way. Help him beat the simulator one last time!

## ITEMS

**Health Pickup**
Restore some health to a damaged craft.

**Missile Pickup**
Allows you to fire missiles.

**Shield Pickup**
Gives you extra shielding for a short period of time.

**Rapid Fire Pickup**
For a limited time, allows you to continuously fire shots.

**Double Shot Pickup**
For a limited time, fire a pair of energy blasts with each shot.

## PS2

| | |
|---|---|
| ● | Shoot |
| ● (held down) | Shoot continuously while Rapid Fire Pickup is active |
| ● | Missile (After Missile Pickup) |
| L1 | Tilt Left |
| R1 | Tilt Right |

## GC

| | |
|---|---|
| ● | Shoot |
| ● (held down) | Shoot continuously while Rapid Fire Pickup is active |
| | Missile (After Missile Pickup) |
| | Tilt Left |
| | Tilt Right |

## XBOX

| | |
|---|---|
| ● | Shoot |
| ● (held down) | Shoot continuously while Rapid Fire Pickup is active |
| ● | Missile (After Missile Pickup) |
| L | Tilt Left |
| R | Tilt Right |

## DANGERS

Don't collide with the objects and buildings floating by.

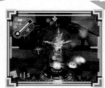

Avoid enemy fire, as well as the enemy ships.

Stay away from the mothership's three defenses.

## Third-Time's the Charm

The head-on style of the first simulator mission is back, but this time the ship travels through the very heart of the planet. When the action begins, you're traveling toward an opening in the side of the planet. There's one asteroid in your path, and a turret at the top and bottom of the entrance. Either shoot down the turret or dodge their fire as you fly in through the opening.

Just a short distance inside the entrance is another gun to the right. Shoot or avoid it, and then shoot apart two bits of debris that block your flight path. The left one reveals a Missile Pickup, while the right gives you a Rapid Fire Pickup. Fly under or over a bar of stone across the way (destroying solid rock takes too long), and watch out for another gun on the left and a few asteroids before a gate to the right holding a Health Pickup.

Just after the gate, a space mine appears. Shoot it down before it can cling to your ship and explode, and it reveals a Shield Pickup. Fly over some pieces of concrete at the bottom of the screen, and watch out for the next bar of stone crossing your path. Go over or under it quickly. After another gun at the bottom and another bar of stone going straight across the path, another stone        juts from the bottom left of the tunnel to the upper right. There's a **card** over it if you're quick enough to fly up and between the ceiling and stone. You may need to tilt your ship slightly to the left to avoid being caught in the rock.

Next, shoot out some more space debris clogging the way to reveal two Health Pickups, and avoid the fire from another gun at the top of the tunnel. Break apart the upcoming bits of debris for more Rapid Fire Pickups and another Missile Pickup, and then destroy some of the upcoming asteroids for a chance at a Health Pickup or two. Watch out for more debris blocking the entire tunnel, and use a missile if needed to take them out of your path in time.

After another turret fires upon you from the right, fly to the upper right to catch another gate and a Health Pickup. Next, you fly into the heart of the planet and the enemy base. A field of asteroids makes progress tricky. In the process, avoid the enemy gunfire from the buildings nearby. Before entering the next tunnel, you fly past a last building with a bit of debris hanging down from its base. Blast this apart for another Health Pickup.

As you sweep into the tunnel, be ready to blast apart a few obstructing bits of debris, especially the one at the upper-right that holds the next **card**. Fly down and catch a gate in the center of the path, with yet another Health Pickup.

Next, you fly into a more constricting tunnel with a bar of stone going across from side to side. Avoid this, and then fly under or between two bits of concrete jutting from the ceiling. Next, you have another concrete obstruction. You can fly down the center with no trouble, or you can take a smaller hole at the top by tilting to one side, picking up a **card** in the process.

To the upper-left, just behind the large concrete obstruction, you find another space mine and scattered asteroids. Past a few more bits of debris, including another set of the paired objects with a Shield Pickup and a Rapid Fire Pickup, you reach another gate and a Health Pickup in the center of the tunnel. You then sweep into a metal and concrete tunnel, choked with debris and weaponry.

Watch the turret at the very start of this manmade tunnel, and sweep to the left side to destroy a vertical piece of debris. This releases a Rapid Fire Pickup along with the next **card**. Blast apart as much of the other debris as you can, because it may drop various random pickups. When you fly into a larger open space, concentrate your fire on a globe in the center of a device. Fly in through the same area, and then go back into the tunnel.

This next tunnel is also choked with debris holding various pickups, including three objects that completely block the tunnel just a short way in. If you can't shoot the debris out of the way quick enough, use a missile or two. Then you need to weave in and out of the metal poles jutting across part of the narrow tunnel, shooting asteroids as you go for a chance at a health pickup. The next gate, holding a Health Pickup, is to the upper-left of the narrow part of the tunnel.

Just after the gate, swing up and to the right to pick up another **card**, partially obstructed by a large asteroid. Then make your way out into free space. The mothership appears, although you cannot act until it gets into position in front of you and its health bar appears on the upper-right corner of the screen.

To win this fight, you must deplete the health of four red panels on the ship, each panel making up one-fourth of the overall health of the ship. Regular fire will work, although missiles are quicker. After you destroy one target, you automatically fly to the next. Of course, each panel is protected by different defenses. If at any point your ship is destroyed while fighting this foe, you return to a point just before fighting the mothership. It's good that you don't have to repeat the whole level, but you're limited to 10 missiles.

This first target sends out long chains of energy shots every few seconds. At first they're in a straight line across the screen, which you can avoid by just flying over or under them. As the enemy's health bar gets lower, they start to appear in a cross, stretching from side to side and from top to bottom. These are harder to avoid. You must fly to one corner of the screen as far as you can, and then swing back in to take a few more shots at the target before avoiding the next round of fire.

When the health bar for the mothership is down by one-fourth, the panel is destroyed and you move down and to the left. This next panel is protected by streams of liquid-like energy that come out of two small holes beside the target. At first, just the lower-left hole emits the energy, but as the target's health drops, it starts to release energy from both holes at the same time. Try to gauge where each stream is heading, and dodge into an empty space until the energy dies down. Then go back to shooting.

With this second target down, you sweep over to the right side of the ship to repeat the process. This time you're fired upon by missiles, which appear from the sides of the target and step up their pace as you bring the target's health down further. Keep an eye out for these missiles, and dodge to the side as they come closer. When you hear a tone and the crosshairs marking a missile turn red, it means that the missile is just about to home in on you. Once this third target is destroyed, your ship's health is restored and you move up to the center of the mothership for the final target.

This last target is the most dangerous, because it uses both the streams of energy and the missiles from the second and third panels. You must dodge around the streams of liquid energy as they appear, at the same time keeping an eye out for missiles and hoping you have someplace left to dodge to. Try not to get trapped in any corners, giving yourself as much free space to maneuver as possible. Do most of your attacking during the brief periods when the streams of energy disappear, although you still have to watch out for the missiles.

If you have any missiles left over, this is the time to use them. A steady stream of missiles can take the enemy's health down in a matter of seconds. Once this last target's health reaches zero, your objective is completed, and you emerge victorious over the computer yet again.

# Final Boss

As the title suggests, this is the last major enemy that Chicken Little has to face in order to save his father and keep the town safe from harm. Once he spots a vending machine and uses one last bottle of pop as a rocket, guide the young rooster through the tunnels leading to the final confrontation. Then use everything you've learned to help Chicken Little put the enemy in its place... for good!

## PS2

- ⊗ Jump
- ⊗⊗ Double Jump
- ◯ Slingshot (Hold to aim, release to fire)
- ▢ Yo-yo Attack
- ▢ Yo-yo Swing
- ▢ (Held) Powershot

## GC

- Ⓐ Jump
- ⒶⒶ Double Jump
- Ⓧ Slingshot (Hold to aim, release to fire)
- ● Yo-yo Attack
- ● Yo-yo Swing
- ● (Held) Powershot

## XBOX

- ● Jump
- ●● Double Jump
- ● Slingshot (Hold to aim, release to fire)
- ● Yo-yo Attack
- ●● Yo-yo Swing
- ⑦ (Held) Powershot

## DANGERS

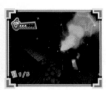

Avoid the obstructions inside the starting tunnels, including glass pipes and large pieces of debris from the town.

Avoid the laser fire and energy bombs from the final boss.

Dodge the enemy fire from the guns stationed toward the end of the tunnel.

Don't fall from the edges of the final fight area.

# Flight of Fancy

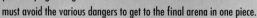

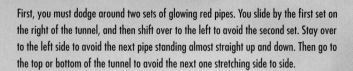

Before the final confrontation starts, you have to get there in the first place. Luckily there's a vending machine handy, so Chicken Little gets a boost from a bottle of soda and flies through the ship at rocket speeds. At the start of the mission, you're flying through narrow tunnels and must avoid the various dangers to get to the final arena in one piece.

First, you must dodge around two sets of glowing red pipes. You slide by the first set on the right of the tunnel, and then shift over to the left to avoid the second set. Stay over to the left side to avoid the next pipe standing almost straight up and down. Then go to the top or bottom of the tunnel to avoid the next one stretching side to side.

After the first four obstructions, you fly into a more open area, littered with debris from the attack on the town. Fly over the first very large piece in your path, catching the first **card** along the way. Immediately shift far to the right to avoid the next piece of debris, and then far to the left for the next piece. If you smash into one of these large pieces of debris, not only do you lose an egg, but chances are you'll keep smashing into it, unable to move over in time to get past, until all of your eggs are gone.

Now fly down toward the center of the last big piece of debris, and go through the small tunnel in the center to get to the other side. Past the debris, dodge to the left and then right to avoid two more sets of the red glass pipes. Then fly through a checkpoint, saving your progress along the tunnel so far.

77

Now you have three revolving fans to slip past. Since it's hard to judge their speed and rotation as you're rushing toward them, it's best to just pick one spot on the very edge of the tunnel and stay there, hoping you slip past all the fans. If you get past the first one with a lot of space to spare, you can most likely stay in the same spot to miss the next two. If it's a close call, change your position slightly to give yourself a better shot at getting through unscathed.

After the fans, you fly into a more open section with turrets on each side shooting at you. After each wave of shots, change your position, avoiding the next shots as they home in on your earlier location. Watch the way the shots are heading, and dodge to another spot if you must.

Past the turrets, you fly into another section with a lot of glass pipes. Fly far to the left side of the tunnel to avoid the first set, and then hug the ceiling of the tunnel for the next. Immediately fly down to the bottom to bypass the third set, and stay there to fly past the single pipe stretching across the tunnel. Shift to the left to fly past another single pipe stretching top to bottom. Then move to the top-left corner to bypass a pipe stretching diagonally, and pick up the second **card** hanging over it.

As soon as you're past this last pipe, you fly into another open section. Land here before facing one more large menace.

# The Big Showdown

This final boss fight consists of three stages, each one more difficult than the last. To start with, you're on the bottom ring of a circular area. The Final Boss you must fight is in the center, while you're free to move all around him. Don't get too close to the edge near the enemy, or you slip off and fall, losing an egg.

Your arena for this fight is scattered with various objects. The smaller blue objects that look like cans of paint each contain an acorn, so start breaking them open with your yo-yo if you need a few more eggs. Just be careful when you do this. The boss can sometimes home in on the sound and make you a target.

Be careful around the larger, greenish-blue objects scattered around the floor, and don't stand close to them for long. These are explosive. They don't damage you directly, but they explode and take out a section of floor whenever they're in the way of the boss's firepower or you attack them. This leaves gaps that you must jump over. If you fall through, you lose another egg.

The final object is a red-lit crate holding a **card**. At the start of the fight, run just to the left to get behind this crate, and wait for the foe to charge up a shot and fire. The crate blocks all of the shot so you don't need to dodge, and in the process it breaks open, freeing the card for you to collect.

The Final Boss itself is a large circular weapon on a central pole. It can move up and down, and swivels around to face any point in the circle. At the front it has a laser, which it charges with a red glow before firing its strongest attack for this round. It attacks when it senses you in front of it, whenever you strike its body with an acorn from your slingshot, and sometimes when you attack objects nearby to break them open. If you keep running around the circle, its shots fly harmlessly behind you. Just don't get stuck on an object in your path, or fall off the edge of a gap.

The Final Boss also has two red switches, one on each side of the gun. When you hit one of these with an acorn from your slingshot, it turns green. This isn't extremely difficult in this first stage. Although the enemy moves around a lot, it stops moving after it fires off one of its charged shots. This gives you a chance to run around to the side, aim, and fire. After hitting a switch, move as soon as you can. The Final Boss homes in on you, fires off one quick shot immediately, and then charges up a stronger shot as it swivels to follow your movements.

Once both switches are green, the enemy stops, swivels to one side, and sends out a glowing bulb-shaped object on the floor along the circular walkway. Attack this bulb while you can, either with your slingshot or a yo-yo attack. Each time you hit it (if it's not enough to finish it off), the bulb is pulled up and away, and it sets down a bit farther along the circle. If you don't destroy this object within a short time, it gets pulled back into the enemy and you have to start aiming for the switches again.

Another important difference is that the enemy also shoots off blue "bombs" of energy that soar up high and come down to damage anything nearby. You need to watch where they're heading and avoid being too close when they land. The boss only tends to shoot these off when it can't find you to take a charged laser shot. So if it starts to use the bombs, hit the foe with a quick acorn to grab its attention again. Be especially careful if you're sitting behind the card crate. This can make you a sitting duck.

Once the object takes enough damage—two or three slingshot hits, or one good Powershot strike—the Final Boss shudders, any remaining "paint cans" around the circle break open, and the enemy shifts up to the higher level. Run around and collect any acorns you haven't already picked up. Then find a spot where a platform is now rising from the floor and hop on.

The final big difference is that this time, the sides of the turret swivel around in a slow circle as well. This means that when the Final Boss is holding still, you may have to wait

for a switch to come into position before you fire at it. You probably need to spend longer catching the boss's attention, having it shoot off a charged laser, and then hoping you can trigger the switches in time, especially if you've already turned one green and it's currently facing you.

Walkthrough

To one side of the platform as it rises counterclockwise around the circle, you see a set of three platforms acting like steps. Jump to them, and jump along each step to reach a swing. Leap out, latch onto it with your yo-yo, and swing onto another platform. From the other end of this platform, you find another swing, which in turn leads to another set of three platform steps. At the other end you jump to another rising platform, and then to a second.

When you've finished this second stage, repeat the process from before. Collect the last acorns, and then find the platform and ride on it, this time until you can jump to a trampoline. From the trampoline, jump to a platform, and from there, use the two swings to reach another set of platform steps leading up.

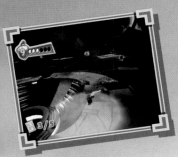

From here you jump on a trampoline, grab onto a swing, repeat the process with another trampoline and swing, and finally land on a platform. Run to the other end and double jump up into the air, then latch onto a line in the air with your yo-yo. Slide down this line to the next platform, which takes you up to the third stage. Unfortunately, this time you only collect five acorns on the climb between stages, but chances are you've managed to collect a lot more after the fight.

As this platform rises higher, you can jump to another set of two platforms. At the end of this set, you reach a different type of platform. Jump to it and it rises up to the next level, taking you back to the boss fight. On the bright side, the entire chain taking you up from the first rising platform to the next stage of the fight contains 13 acorns, giving you more than enough for another egg.

The second stage of the fight is much like the first, but there are a few key differences. First, and most superficial, is that the crate containing the fourth **card** is across the circle. You must run to it the long way around, and then get the enemy's attention by shooting off an acorn at it or something similar, before ducking behind the crate and letting it be destroyed.

Once again, the Final Boss's switch rotation is slightly different. While they still turn at a steady pace, this time they move much more quickly. This makes it a lot more difficult to hit the switch at just the right time, without striking the Final Boss's body by mistake.

The other change concerns the weapon the Final Boss uses once it homes in on you. Although the enemy sometimes still uses a normal charged laser when it spots you, most of the time it charges slightly, jerks away, and then sweeps a large area with a narrow laser beam along the floor. There's no way to avoid this by just running away. Wait for the robot to move slightly away, and then jump as soon as it starts to fire the laser. A double jump is even safer. You may get hit the first time or two as you learn the precise timing.

This time the **card** is in a crate far away from your starting position, but the sweeping laser breaks it open. Many of the acorns are also broken open by this weapon and scattered around the floor, making them easier to collect without attracting the attention of the boss if you need a boost.

As soon as you destroy the enemy for the third time, you're prompted to save your game. The mission is over. Now you just have two more missions remaining.

# Runt's Escape

After you've defeated the final boss, there's a quick confrontation. And with that, most of the problems seem to be solved. Except no one's told the other friends! Help Runt as he drives the trusty firetruck through the alien corridors, searching for the door to the outside world and a handy escape.

## PS2

| | |
|---|---|
| ✕ | Accelerate |
| ◯ | Brake |
| △ | Reverse |
| L1 | Powerslide |
| L2 | Powerslide |

## GC

| | |
|---|---|
| A | Accelerate |
| B | Brake |
| | Reverse |
| | Powerslide |
| | Powerslide |

## XBOX

| | |
|---|---|
| | Accelerate |
| | Brake |
| | Reverse |
| L | Powerslide |
| R | Powerslide |

## ITEMS

Clock — Driving through this adds five seconds to your countdown.

## DANGERS

If you run out of time on the clock, you have to start the race over again.

Driving off the path into open space or other open areas also forces you to start again.

## Run for the Exit!

There are no checkpoints on this trip. You've got to make it through all at once, or not at all. This is another run that starts with a short time limit. In this mission you collect alarm clocks that add extra time to your clock, while racing as fast as you can toward the exit. If you ever get turned around, a warning shows up, telling you that you're going the wrong way.

For the most part, you want to just mash down the Accelerate button (normally the jump button) to keep speeding up as you move through the ship. Unless you're coming to an especially dangerous curve, don't ease up or even brake. If you smash into something head-on, you may have to reverse to get back to the right path. But in general, keep moving, even if it means you miss a clock or two. You lose more time going back for a missed pickup than if you keep moving without it.

You start out at one end of a corridor with 20 seconds on the clock. Drive straight forward, accelerating as you go, to nab the first clock. Then start bearing left to squeeze around the upcoming obstacles in the path. The right side has a few extra objects at the edge, and it's a bit harder to get around safely. Make sure you get back to the center of the hall in time to pick up a second clock.

The next section consists of many solid obstacles in the center, changing between two to the side and then one in the center, also with a clear path to each side. If you're terrible at steering, take one of the side paths, but the best choice is to head for the center. Weave between two objects, to the side of the one in the center, and then back toward the center for the next two, and so on. This method also gains you the first **card**, which is tucked away between two of the objects, as well as a clock toward the end.

Now you head onto a clear ramp that turns to the left, with clocks on the right, left, and then right. Be careful as you steer. Driving off the side of the ramp forces you to start over. As the path straightens out, another clock appears to the left, and then one to the center just before you travel through objects moving along lines across the road.

Watch the movements of these objects closely. You must steer around them, because if one hits you in the side, it almost always knocks you off the ramp and forces you to start the run over. Aim for one of the objects or just behind it, so that you're going through empty space by the time you reach the lines. There are two lines spaced somewhat far apart, followed by two more close together, all moving from left to right.

As soon as you pass the last moving line, make sure you're in the dead center of the ramp and traveling straight. You now hit a large glowing shape in the floor. This acts as launching pad, sending you up higher into the air. You leap over the upcoming empty space and crash through the field into the next corridor. The jump across the gap also holds the second **card**, which you should collect if you're moving at the right speed and in the right direction.

Then you come to a hallway that's set up much like the area where you collected the first card. There are red barricades set up, two together, and then one in the center, alternating. The main difference is that these barriers burst open if you hit them, although they still slow you down. Weave through these as you would the other objects, and collect four clocks total here. There's one clock in each center space that you go through. As you collect the fourth clock, make sure you're driving straight down the center again. You catch another launching pad, although this one only speeds you up, so it isn't quite as necessary.

There are three flimsy barricades blocking the path, although you can bust through them easily even if you miss the launch pad. This brings you to another set of barricades. They're set up just like before, down to the clocks in the centers, but this time there are also the flimsier barriers set up to each side of the single center barriers. Crash through them and just keep your rhythm going, ignoring the impacts as best you can.

After this set of barriers comes another pad, this one taking you over another gap. You can collect a clock in the middle of the jump if you hit it just right. The next hallway has two clocks in a row, the second in one of the breakaway barriers. Then you should swerve to one side to avoid a red barricade. Weave back and forth around the red barricades and back to the center to collect more clocks in the breakaway barriers, until you reach the next launching pad.

This pad just speeds you up. Make sure you veer toward the right after you take it, so you catch the next **card** just before another launch pad. Now you have more solid objects, set up in the same pattern as before—two along the sides, and then one in the center. Just crash through the breakaway barriers scattered along the sides, and center. Then you take another launch pad, this time over another gap.

You reach a streamlined area with a second launching pad to speed you up, followed by a clock toward the right. Back over to the left, you hit another launch pad, and there's another clock on that side. To the right is a launch pad, this time followed by a clock to the left. Then aim for the center as the road straightens out, and you come to one more launching pad. This sends you up through various lines of larger moving objects, a bit easier to see and avoid. Then you hit another launch pad, another clock in the center, and more of the same for a short distance.

After a few moments, you reach a more mechanized section, with giant cogs and energy bursts all around. Watch for a **card** to appear to the right just as the path curves left slightly, and then aim for the center again to go through a doorway and catch the next clock. Stay down the center to jump a ramp into one last stretch of road between various crystals, watching for the final **card** in the center of the path. Then drive straight out into open space, between what appear to be giant teeth guarding the exit out of the spaceship.

# Space Armada

The good deeds are all done, the day is saved, and Chicken Little is now a hero to his hometown of Oakey Oaks and to the world at large. Of course, now the town gets to wait and see what the media makes of this whole event, including the inevitable movie based (roughly) on real events. As an encore, guide the ship of "Chicken Little" through ranks of invading aliens to defeat them all and save the day... again.

## PS2

| | |
|---|---|
| ● | Shoot |
| ● (held down) | Shoot continuously while Rapid Fire Pickup is active. |
| ▲ | Missile (After Missile Pickup) |
| L1 | Tilt Left |
| R1 | Tilt Right |

## GC

| | |
|---|---|
| ● | Shoot |
| ● (held down) | Shoot continuously while Rapid Fire Pickup is active. |
| Y | Missile (After Missile Pickup) |
| | Tilt Left |
| | Tilt Right |

## XBOX

| | |
|---|---|
| ● | Shoot |
| ● (held down) | Shoot continuously while Rapid Fire Pickup is active. |
| ● | Missile (After Missile Pickup) |
| L | Tilt Left |
| R | Tilt Right |

## DANGERS

Avoid crashing into obstacles while flying through space.

Watch out for enemy ships and enemy fire!

## ITEMS

 **Health Pickup**
Restore some health to a damaged craft.

 **Rapid Fire Pickup**
For a limited time, allows you to continuously fire shots.

 **Double Shot Pickup**
Fire paired energy blasts with each shot for a limited time.

 **Missile Pickup**
Allows you to fire missiles.

 **Shield Pickup**
Gives you extra shielding for a short period of time.

# Encore!

Now you get to go out in a final blaze of glory, playing the part of a very glorified "Chicken Little" as he goes out to save the world using his very own spacecraft. The setup and controls of this mission are similar to the "Space Simulator" chapters, although this time the ship looks different.

You start out with 10 missiles and a gauge to keep track of the alien ships you've blasted down. At the very beginning, you're flying straight toward an asteroid field as alien ships dart around between the rocks in front of you. Keep up as steady a rate of fire as you can, and try to knock out as many ships as possible. Of course, you must also dodge around to keep out of the aliens' line of fire at the same time.

When you blow up an enemy ship, it releases either a Missile Pickup or a Rapid Fire Pickup. The latter is especially useful, letting you keep up a more constant stream of fire and giving you a better chance to knock out even more ships.

After sailing through the asteroid field for a while, you fly into an enclosed space. One of the first things you see is a sort of tower, with a section in the center that you can blow apart. Attack it until it explodes, and then pick up your first **card** inside. Then fly down through the next opening into more empty space, knocking out some nearby asteroids for a possible health pickup.

Out in empty space, you fly slowly toward a large, circular red window that looks much like the switches you've hit in the past. Blast it open with a steady stream of fire to reveal a tunnel behind it. Don't ignore the ships firing around you, either. Divide your attention between targets. Fly into the tunnel and out the other side, where another swarm of enemy ships greet you.

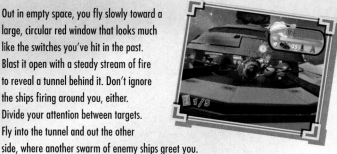

Concentrate on shooting down more ships for a while. Then, as you enter the next tunnel, watch the laser in front of you, moving quickly from right to left. You want to gauge your crossing carefully. Speed yourself through at just the right time to miss the laser. Do the same for the next laser moving from the top to the bottom of the tunnel, and you're once again in open space.

Walkthrough

Then you're in another asteroid field. Blast the bad guys, as well as the asteroids for the pickups they may reveal. As you approach a large station spinning in orbit, aim for one hole in its rim that holds a second **card**, before getting back to more of the asteroid field.

As you approach the underside of some heavy rock formations, you must twist and turn between them. First go to the right and fly into a narrow arch in the rock to collect the next **card**, and then shift to the left to collect the fourth **card**. Then you approach a narrow crack in the rock, which is your only escape. Aim for one of the slightly larger sections of the crack, and tilt your craft to one side to slip through and back out into free space.

83

You run into more enemies, this time firing a bit more heavily at your ship. You may find Health Pickups in the asteroids, which is useful if you take too many hits. Eventually, you reach a tunnel guarded by a door that starts to close as you approach. Use your thrust to get through it before it shuts. Travel down the tunnel and out the opposite door when it opens, and then fly up while tilting your ship to one side to pluck the last **card** out from between two pieces of metal.

Then you reach the last section of your journey, filled with alien spacecraft and an asteroid field. You can still get the various pickups here, which is good because the rate of fire of the bad guys speeds up once again, and you may take some heavy hits. You must also watch out for larger craft that appear occasionally, more often toward the end of your flight. These send out heftier attacks of energy and are more dangerous, but they eventually fly off past you into the distance.

After a long time under the assault of the bad guys, you run into one last deadly formation of enemies. Shoot down as many of them as you can, as quickly as possible, and fly through the fields of checkered lines that mark the finish line. Now your objective is complete, and so is your game!

# General Store

You can visit the General Store at any point in between chapters to purchase upgrades for the story, dodgeball, or racing. Use acorns to make your purchase.

## Story

### HEALTH UPGRADES (COST IN ACORNS)

| CHARACTER | 1 | 2 | 3 |
|---|---|---|---|
| Chicken Little | 100 | 200 | 300 |
| Commander Ace | 100 | 200 | 300 |
| Fish out of Water | 100 | 200 | 300 |

## Dodgeball

### UNIFORMS (COST IN ACORNS)

| CHARACTER | UNLOCK | RED UNIFORM | BLUE UNIFORM | ORANGE UNIFORM | WHITE UNIFORM |
|---|---|---|---|---|---|
| Chicken Little | — | 100 | 200 | 300 | 500 |
| Foxy Loxy | — | 100 | 200 | 300 | 500 |
| Abby | 2000 | | | | |
| Runt | 2500 | | | | |
| Commander Ace | 4000 | | | | |

You can also buy new dodgeball colors for 25 acorns each—Red, Beach, 3-color, or Black. You can also buy uniforms for Abby, Runt and Ace, too.

## Race

### CLUCK MOBILE UPGRADES (COST IN ACORNS)

| UPGRADE TYPE | 1 | 2 | 3 | 4 | 5 |
|---|---|---|---|---|---|
| Red, Blue, Green Paint | 25 (each) | | | | |
| Motor | 100 | 200 | 300 | 400 | 500 |
| Tire | 50 | 100 | 150 | 200 | 250 |
| Frame | 75 | 150 | 225 | 300 | 375 |

### FISH TANKER UPGRADES (COST IN ACORNS)

| UPGRADE TYPE | 1 | 2 | 3 | 4 | 5 |
|---|---|---|---|---|---|
| Red, Dark Blue, Green Paint | 25 (each) | | | | |
| Motor | 100 | 200 | 300 | 400 | 500 |
| Tire | 50 | 100 | 150 | 200 | 250 |
| Frame | 75 | 150 | 225 | 300 | 375 |

### FIRE TRUCK UPGRADES (COST IN ACORNS)

| UPGRADE TYPE | 1 | 2 | 3 | 4 | 5 |
|---|---|---|---|---|---|
| Orange, Blue, Green Paint | 25 (each) | | | | |
| Motor | 100 | 200 | 300 | 400 | 500 |
| Tire | 50 | 100 | 150 | 200 | 250 |
| Frame | 75 | 150 | 225 | 300 | 375 |

### TURKEY LIMO UPGRADES (COST IN ACORNS)

| UPGRADE TYPE | 1 | 2 | 3 | 4 | 5 |
|---|---|---|---|---|---|
| Unlock | 1000 | | | | |
| Motor | 100 | 200 | 300 | 400 | 500 |
| Tire | 50 | 100 | 150 | 200 | 250 |
| Frame | 75 | 150 | 225 | 300 | 375 |

### SCHOOL BUS UPGRADES (COST IN ACORNS)

| UPGRADE TYPE | 1 | 2 | 3 | 4 | 5 |
|---|---|---|---|---|---|
| Red, Blue, Grey Paint | 25 (each) | | | | |
| Motor | 100 | 200 | 300 | 400 | 500 |
| Tire | 50 | 100 | 150 | 200 | 250 |
| Frame | 75 | 150 | 225 | 300 | 375 |

### RUNT SPACESHIP UPGRADES (COST IN ACORNS)

| UPGRADE TYPE | 1 | 2 | 3 | 4 | 5 |
|---|---|---|---|---|---|
| Unlock | 1500 | | | | |
| Motor | 100 | 200 | 300 | 400 | 500 |
| Tire | 50 | 100 | 150 | 200 | 250 |
| Frame | 75 | 150 | 225 | 300 | 375 |

# Minigames

When you start your Game Boy Advance with the CHICKEN LITTLE game inserted, you have a choice of five different selections. One is the main story mode, covered in the walkthrough. You can also check music, animations or change the game options. The last two options are mini-games that you can play for fun and to increase your acorns.

The two mini-games available are Dodgeball and Racing. You can buy improvements for each using acorns at the General Store, and you can also unlock a few new options just by winning games.

## Dodgeball

Defeat all three characters inside the opposing team's half of the court.
**REWARD:**
25 Acorns

## GBA

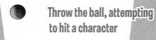

Ⓐ  Pass the ball

Ⓑ  Throw the ball, attempting to hit a character

Ⓡ  Switch targets

The purpose of dodgeball probably needs little explanation—there are two teams, and each team attempts to strike the other players with the ball, knocking them out of the game. The last team left wins the game. There are a few twists to this version though which require a bit of explanation.

Once you select the "Dodgeball" option from the main menu screen, you are given a chance to choose your location, your team captain, the jerseys you wear, and the actual ball you use. Some of these options become available as you win more and more games, while others are upgrades that you buy at the General Store. Select "Start" at the bottom when you're ready.

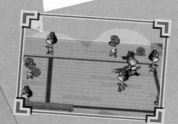

First off, your team consists of six players, but only three are within your side of the court and able to be picked off. The other three are on the edge of the other team's side of the court. Your job is to pass the ball back and forth by pressing A, using B to try to pick off one of the other three team members inside their half-court when you think you have a good shot lined up. You also have to avoid shots from the other team members surrounding your own half of the court.

Once the game gets underway, watch the different colored circles for some key information. Green marks the character on your team currently carrying the ball, or targeted by the enemy. Blue marks your own next target among your own teammates, while a red circle shows who your target on the opposing team is. You can switch enemy targets by pressing the Right Shoulder button, while your target on your own team is determined by the direction buttons as you make your throw.

If an opposing team member throws the ball at you, press B and face the ball to try to catch it. If you do catch it, you take no damage. If you miss and the ball hits you, you lose part of your bar of health. The same holds true for the opposite team members. To have a better chance of knocking them out, try using A to pass to one of the team members on the sidelines around the enemy's court, although you have to be careful not to let the pass get intercepted. Then try a shot at an opposing character from close range, while their backs are turned.

Once all three members of one team have been taken out of the game by losing all of their health, the surviving team wins the match. If you manage to win, you collect 50 acorns.

# Racing

**Race around four laps as quickly as possible, coming in first for the best result**

**REWARD:**

**Varies by place (first place wins 250 acorns)**

## ITEMS

**Tools**
These items repair your car a bit, making it reach its potential more easily.

**Turbo**
Pick up one of these items to restore a bit of energy to your turbo gauge.

## GBA

 **Accelerate**

 **Brake**

 **Turbo**

Like dodgeball, racing needs little explanation. Here you control one of four vehicles in a race, and you need to make four laps around a course. Your place at the end of the race determines how many acorns you get as a reward. In addition there are more acorns scattered around the race track, with Tools and Turbo recharges to pick up as well.

To start the racing game, select "Race" from the main menu and then select your vehicle and the race track. Race tracks unlock as you win more races, while you can unlock more vehicles and improve them through the General Store.

On the race screen, you can watch your current engine performance by looking at the colored meter at the top left of the screen. To the right of this meter you find your turbo meter, with your current speed below it. Each turbo recharge adds three dots back to your turbo meter, but this cannot go above the maximum. At the top of the screen you see your current place in the group, while the currently collected acorns are to the far right. At the bottom left corner you see a mini-map showing the general course shape, and the placement of each vehicle.

During the race itself, a key to winning is to get into first and stay there, which lowers your collisions with other cars and gives you a clear shot at the pickups. Make good use of your turbo, as this increases your speed and you can replenish it at random by picking up the lightning-bolt shaped symbols along the track. Just make sure you don't collide with other vehicles or the sides of the course, as this slows you down!

Once you cross the finish line after your fourth lap the race is finished, and you go to the screen showing your final placement, and you receive acorns both as a reward for your placement, and those that you picked up over the course of the race.

# Story Introduction

Much like the "home console" versions of the game, the version of CHICKEN LITTLE for the Game Boy Advance follows in the footsteps of the movie, but with a slightly different spin on things. The action takes place more as a two-dimensional platformer, where you must direct one of three characters throughout various levels and reach the goal at the end, collecting items along the way.

Each time you leave the screen, such as when you fall through a gap or into sludge, you reappear at the start of the obstacle. In other words, at the starting edge of the particular lake you're trying to cross, the ledge you fell from, or something similar. If you take enough damage to wipe out your entire egg meter you start again at the beginning of the particular section you're on. Each chapter usually holds three or four sections.

Whenever you see the Save icon appear at the bottom of the screen, it means your game is being saved. This happens whenever you finish a chapter, complete a mini-game, or visit the General Store. Each game is saved into one of three save files, so you can have up to three games going at the same time before having to delete one.

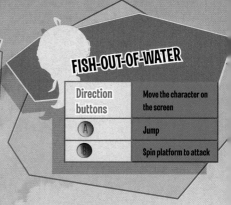

## Controls

Controls within each section of the game differ to some extent, but here are some of the more common:

### CHICKEN LITTLE

| | |
|---|---|
| Direction buttons | Move the character on the screen |
| A | Jump |
| B | Attack/Use yoyo |
| B (Held, then released) | Power shot |
| B + Down | Spin in place |
| B + Down while jumping | A head-first dive toward the ground |
| R | Use a bottle of soda (when available) |

### COMMANDER "ACE" LITTLE

| | |
|---|---|
| Direction buttons | Move the character on the screen |
| A | Jump |
| A (while already jumping) | Double jump |
| B | Attack (fists, or a gun when one is equipped) |
| L | Change between the two guns (when both have been collected) |

### FISH-OUT-OF-WATER

| | |
|---|---|
| Direction buttons | Move the character on the screen |
| A | Jump |
| B | Spin platform to attack |

There are additional hints on using your controls throughout the walkthrough chapters themselves.

# Items

Each section of the game has its own items to use or collect, but those listed here are extremely important to the game and how it works.

## corns

In this version of the game, acorns are collected throughout each chapter, or awarded at the end of a successful mini-game. They are the "currency" for the game—after you collect a number of acorns, go to the General Store and trade some in for various improvements.

There are three types of acorn—green, silver, and gold. Green acorns count as one, silver give you five, and gold acorns are worth ten. The silver and gold are rarer, and you often have to look in out-of-the-way places to collect them.

## ggs

Eggs are sometimes found in your normal pathway during a scenario, and sometimes in hidden places such as inside the bulb of a lamp, which you must break in order to collect.

These items are important, because Chicken Little and Commander Ace each have an "egg meter" that acts as their health. Each time they take damage, they lose an egg. Picking up a normal egg during a chapter restores one point on their egg meter, while picking up a large egg restores all the eggs on their meter at once.

## ish Food

This item is the same as an egg, but used by Fish during his time in the spotlight.

## Golden "Ace" Statue

These items are collectible and are the reward for discovering one of the harder-to-find areas in the level.

# Using the Walkthrough

Each chapter in this guide's game walkthrough covers one level in the game itself. For this particular version of the game the chapters aren't covered in great detail, but the screenshots and captions can give you some help in getting through the trickier spots, or in locating or obtaining some of the slightly harder items. There are also a few listings at the top of each walkthrough section to give you a quick and easy reference to some of the important parts of the level.

## Items

There are items that you pick up or use within the particular chapter, other than the items already covered such as eggs or acorns.

## Dangers

These are the things you need to watch out for in each level that might take away some of your precious eggs. If something is listed here, keep a close watch out for it over the course of the section.

# Cluck House

Chicken Little can't get past the reporters to get to school, so Buck Cluck is willing to take him. Unfortunately, he can't get the garage door open. Before he hurts himself fixing it, Chicken Little has to reset the fuses and get the garage door working again.

You can collect 50 acorns in this level.

## ITEMS

**Yoyo**

You have to collect this before you can use any of the yoyo moves.

**Coin**

Touching one of these shows the next action you should take, and the controls to perform it.

**Fuse**

Flip six fuse switches to turn the power to the garage door back on.

## Around the House

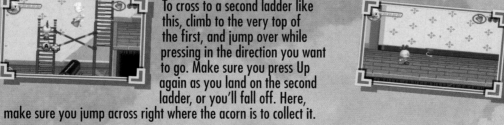

Touch each coin on the level to get a quick control tutorial and see what to do next.

Jump up to the top of the couch by bouncing on your head using Down and B together, and then jump up to collect the green acorns. The silver acorn has to wait.

You can often climb ladder-shaped objects by pressing Up when standing in front of them.

To cross to a second ladder like this, climb to the very top of the first, and jump over while pressing in the direction you want to go. Make sure you press Up again as you land on the second ladder, or you'll fall off. Here, make sure you jump across right where the acorn is to collect it.

Chicken Little's yoyo is your most important tool. Once you pick it up, you can use its attacks for various purposes. Right now this means you can also go back to collect a few out-of-reach acorns.

Go back to one of the stands, jump using A, and press Up + B to shoot your yoyo straight up. You collect the silver acorn when your yoyo touches it.

Press Up + B (to shoot the yo-yo straight up) in the middle of the table for a green acorn...

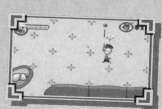

...and from the back of the sofa to collect a silver one.

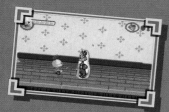

If you can't walk past or jump over an obstacle, try a normal attack to see if you can get past.

If you can't break an obstacle using a normal attack, use a Powershot. Face the obstacle and hold down B, and then release it to attack with a stronger hit.

Bounce from the tabletop and use the Down + B move to leap up higher in the air. Collect two silver acorns, one on each side of the ladder. Then jump up to the ladder and press Up when you reach it to climb into the attic.

In the attic, go left, jump onto the file cabinet, press Up, and attack to flip the first switch. A green light means that the switch is on, which is what you want.

Knock a garbage can onto its side with a yoyo attack…

…and then jump onto it to use it as a springboard. Use the Down + B combination to bounce up higher here and collect a few out-of-reach acorns, including a rare gold one.

Game Boy Advance

Jump onto the objects to the left to reach the second fusebox.

Head back to the right of the ladder and you find the third fusebox within reach.

Pull yourself to the top of the stack of books on the table. Then jump to the left onto a ledge to collect an acorn and hit the fourth fuse.

From the top of the book stack, you can reach a second ledge to the right for another acorn and the fifth fuse.

To turn a screw, faucet, or some other object, jump on top of it and press Down + B to twirl your yoyo around you in a spin. This turns what you're standing on, depending on which direction you're facing when you start the spin. Here, face toward the books, jump up to collect the acorns, and then reach the top of the books when the screw is as high as it goes.

From the top of the book stack, you can also reach the sixth fuse with a yoyo attack.

Once you've flipped all six switches, go to the power button at the right of the attic. Switch it on with a yoyo attack to finish the level.

91

# Town Hall

Unfortunately even with his father's help, Chicken Little has missed the bus to school. Now he has to walk all the way there, avoiding reporters who are hounding him after last year's incident.

You can collect 80 acorns and an Ace statue in this level.

## ITEMS

**Ace Coin**

Touch this to turn into Commander "Ace" Little temporarily, and use his skills to get past obstacles.

## DANGERS

Watch out for the reporters—their cameras send out stars that take away an egg when they take a picture!

In the sewers, don't fall into the nasty slime and sludge.

In the country, jump over the water.

Beware of the branches and leaves falling from trees.

## Fight City Hall!

Whenever you see a garbage can knock it over...

...then use it as a springboard (with the "down" + B head bounce move) to leap up on top of the lamps, which may have acorns overtop of them.

Lamps with bulbs could hold an acorn or and egg—break them open.

Use the "down" + B headbounce on any grates you find...

...and you open a path into a sewer level.

In the sewers, jump over any slime. The barrels floating in the middle of the sludge are good stepping-stones to help you get across to the other side.

Once you reach the other end of the sewers, attack up with your yoyo to open the exit. Don't press up before attacking though, or you climb the ladder.

The floppy-eared dog reporters take two hits with a yoyo to stop. Watch out for their cameras.

Cat reporters can use the same "attack" as the dogs, but they only take one hit before they are stopped for good.

Knock over a half-hidden garbage can toward the back of this car and use it to bounce up onto the hood, where in turn you can bounce up and use "up" and an attack upward to collect a few acorns.

Watch out for the reporters hiding behind the fence. Attack straight up with your yoyo to put them out of business. After passing three reporters you reach the end of the first section.

# ce, Ace, Baby

Back down in the sewers, cross the first slime pit and touch the coin to change into Ace and punch through the first couple gates.

After you spend the time breaking down the first few gates, you soon turn back into Chicken Little. Go back to the coin and trigger it again, and go directly to the right as far as you can to break open one last gate and reach a gold acorn.

Break into the next grate as soon as you can. It is an isolated sewer that has only one entrance, but some interesting items to collect.

Down in the sewers, make sure you wander to the left over a long pit of slime to collect an isolated silver acorn.

Next go back by the steps and use a jump or "up" yoyo attack to trigger the "Ace" coin.

Quickly destroy four gates one after the other to reach the golden statue for the level.

Back up top, knock over the next garbage can you see and use it...

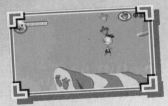

...to bounce up onto the awning, which acts as a trampoline. From here you can collect more acorns overhead.

From the other end of the awning you can also jump out to reach another acorn in mid-air.

There is a single acorn overtop of a traffic signal.

Use a garbage can to bounce onto the high crates partway down the street, but watch out for a reporter on top as soon as you land.

This street lamp by the gray house has especially good items of note. Use a garbage can to bounce up to it.

To reach acorns on taller traffic signals like this, jump up to the shorter "box" on the signal and use it to pull yourself up to the taller portions.

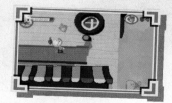

Make sure you bounce up to this striped awning to collect another silver acorn.

# A Stroll in the Countryside

Jump back down to reach a "ledge" further to the right, and make sure you jump down to the fire truck itself to collect this acorn.

To get past the fire truck parked in your way, first climb the ladder into the tree...

...then start to jump between the light green-colored branches; pull yourself up if you need to.

Crossing through tall grass like this slows down your movements. This isn't extremely important right now, but it may throw you off at first.

Whenever you run into a haystack, use a Powershot (hold down B and release) to break through it.

Falling into the water is dangerous. You lose an egg, so leap across each pond you find.

You must be especially careful starting with the second set of lily pads you try to cross—wait until they submerge and come back up before you start to cross.

Whenever you see a conspicuous low-hung branch in your path, approach it but stop before you actually go under it. It falls down as soon as you get close.

Logs like this one travel slowly back and forth along the water, so jump to one when it's within reach, and then ride it as far as you can.

Boarded-up holes are like the sewer grates. Bust them open with a head-shot to climb underground for a while.

Use Commander Ace to break apart the two rocks you find underground and clear the path. Note that there is a golden acorn hanging in mid-air between the two boulders. Use a double-jump or an "up" attack from Chicken Little to collect it.

There is a silver acorn hanging between where the two logs travel on this last pond.

To end this level of the game you only need to approach the school stairs.

# Dodgeball

Now that Chicken Little has finally made it to school, things aren't getting any easier for him. Foxy Loxy is back to her old tricks, and this time she's stolen Chicken Little's precious yoyo. To win it back, you must defeat Foxy in a game of Dodgeball.

## ITEMS

**Yoyo**
You must win a game of Dodgeball to get this precious item back.

## DANGERS

Don't get hit by the dodgeball. Try to either catch it or avoid it altogether.

## Fun and Games

The main players in this game are Chicken Little on the left and Foxy Loxy on the right. The cats surrounding Foxy are on Chicken Little's team, while the dogs are on Foxy's team.

The different-colored circles around the characters mean different things. A green circle marks Chicken Little, or an ally who holds the ball or is a possible target. Red is an enemy target, while blue marks your current target if you pass the ball.

When an opposing team member throws the ball, try to face it and press B to catch it. If you fail and the ball hits you, you lose some points of health. Lose all of your health and you lose the match.

When one of your team members is holding the ball, pass it to another teammate by pressing one of the directions and A. If you're not careful, this throw can be intercepted by Foxy!

Use B to throw the ball at Foxy and try to damage her. To keep her from catching it, throw it when her back is turned. Making one of the cats near her throw it can make it more likely to hit, and more damaging as well.

If you can take down all of Foxy Loxy's health, you win. You get your yoyo back and can move on to the next level.

# Baseball

Chicken Little has joined the baseball team of Oakey Oaks, and he's hoping for a chance to play. He'll never get his turn at the plate, though, if he can't get to the game on time! Once again, Foxy Loxy is trying to ruin the day by blocking Chicken Little's path to the baseball stadium. Help Chicken Little find a path that gets him around Foxy and to the game on time.

You can collect 100 acorns and one Ace statue on this level.

## ITEMS

**Ace Coin**
Touch this to turn into Commander Ace and use his abilities for a time.

## DANGERS

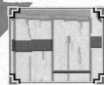
Dodge the fence boards that flip over every so often.

Watch out for the reporters and their cameras.

Stay out of the jets of steam coming from some pipes. Wait for them to die down before you cross.

## Take Me Out to the Ballgame

Make sure you get the silver acorn over the first garbage can.

As you move forward, watch out for the shorter fence boards that stand out a bit. These flip over occasionally, and if they hit you, they take away an egg.

Shortly along the fence, you start running into reporters both on the ground and behind the fence. It may seem easier to just bypass the reporters than to fight with them, but if you break their cameras now, it saves you some hassle later.

This ladder may look tempting, but you just can't reach it quite yet. If ladders are out of your reach like this, it usually means you can get at them later in some way.

When you reach this metal structure, jump toward it and pull yourself up from the edge...

...and then jump from the structure up onto the top of the fence, and start back the way you came.

As you walk back along the fence, be careful of the flipping boards. They can dump you back onto the ground while taking away an egg. If you haven't fought off the reporters, it's especially tough…

…because you have to get close enough to attack them without either running into them or standing on one of the flipping boards. Don't miss the acorns hanging in the air, either!

When you reach the ladder from the top of the fence, go past it at first and continue along to the left. You eventually reach an egg and a silver acorn to collect. Just don't go any farther, or you'll fall off the fence.

Head back to the ladder, and this time climb to the top.

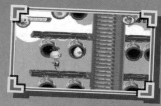

Break open the glass on any telephone poles with your yoyo for possible prizes.

Climb onto the right side of the pole and jump out onto a high-tension wire, which acts much like a long, thin trampoline.

Game Boy Advance

When you reach a straight stretch of wire, bounce high to get a silver acorn in the center. Use a head-bounce to leap up high enough to reach it.

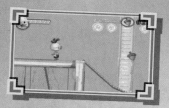

The wire leads to the top of a bulletin board, which leads to another wire…

…which has another silver acorn above the straight part.

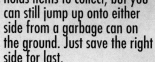

When you reach the next pole and climb down the ladder, you can step onto either the top of the fence or the ground below. The top of the fence holds items to collect, but you can still jump up onto either side from a garbage can on the ground. Just save the right side for last.

The top of the fence to the left holds a normal acorn…

…while the bottom holds a golden acorn. The metal structure you climbed before blocks any further progress to the left.

On top of the fence and to the right, you reach an egg. So if you haven't taken any damage, you don't need to visit this part. Just after the egg, the level ends and you can go no further.

To the right of the last pole, you reach a ladder leading underground (and to the next screen). Climb down once you've collected everything else here.

# Under the Stadium

After climbing down a few ladders, you reach a faucet and a jet of water. Jump on the faucet, face right, and then press Down while hitting B to spin in place and turn the faucet.

After turning the faucet, jump to the top of the jet of water. Ride it up to reach the acorn and the next bit of solid ground.

When you start coming to the various red pipes, watch out for steam coming from some of the holes. If you walk into a jet of steam, it takes away an egg. Wait for the steam to blow out and then die down again before you cross.

When you reach a place where the path forks, first go to the left and collect an acorn, but don't climb down the ladder just yet. Instead, head back along the right/upper path.

When you reach areas with an open space below and a strange grill along the wall, jump up onto the grill and press Up to stick to it like a ladder. Then use the direction buttons to move around in any direction on the grill, collecting any items you find there.

You must also watch out for jets of steam from the pipes set along the floor.

When you reach multiple jets of water that rise to different levels, activate them all and use them as steps to climb to a higher level.

You can also use a jet of water to reach higher on a ladder that you just can't quite reach from below.

Once you reach the Ace coin, use it to turn into Commander Ace. Then double jump up to the jet of water from the faucet, double jump again to reach the next bit of solid ground, and continue to the right.

When you reach the next gate, bash it down. Then head way back to the left to take the lower path you passed up before. You can reach this path with the far-left ladder leading down, or just by falling through one of the various gaps to the section below.

To collect this extra-large egg, crawl carefully below the level of the steam jetting out. To be safe, before you go anywhere near the egg wait for the steam to die down.

When you reach the Ace coin, use it to turn into Ace. Then run right as quickly as you can past the obstacles. Pick up the golden Ace statue, and bash open the nearby gate with your fists before Ace turns back into Chicken Little.

At the top of another ladder, you find two new ladders leading up, with a reporter between them…

…but the left ladder just leads you to the area where the previous upper path meets up with the lower one. If you haven't finished the upper path yet, it's still blocked by a gate.

Up the right ladder and past another faucet and jet of water, you reach another grate against the wall. Wait for the lower jet of steam to shoot up and then die down before you climb past it.

Past the first jet of steam, move to the right to avoid another one from the left, but don't go so far right that you bump into a third jet of steam coming from below. Climb all the way up the grate to reach the end of this screen. Make sure you're finished with the current screen first. After you cross over to the next screen, the gates reappear to block you if you try to come back.

# Foxy Maneuvers

When you come out of the hole onto the next screen, first go left and use the garbage can to bounce up and collect a silver acorn. You cannot jump up onto the nearby roof from here, because the flagpole is in the way.

If you go all the way to the right, you run into Foxy, who will not let you pass.

Instead, go partway between Foxy and the hole you came out of, to where chicken wire acts much like a grate. Press Up to climb onto the wire, and then use the direction buttons to move around.

Watch out for the reporters above the chicken wire. You can't attack them from here, so just wait between reporters for the next one to take a picture, and then move past.

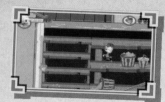

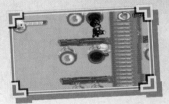

From the chicken wire, you climb onto a roof. Head to the right first, where you find an egg past a nosy reporter.

Back to the left side of the roof, you find another wire to bounce down. There's yet another silver acorn above it, reachable with a head-bounce.

From the next roof, you reach a ladder to climb up another pole.

Toward the top of the pole, watch out for a reporter up on the crossbeams. Jump below him (being careful not to touch him) and attack upward to take him out of the picture.

From the right side of the pole, follow another wire down, and eventually you reach another garbage can. Knock it over and bounce on it to pick up a normal acorn high above…

…and you can also just reach the edge of the roof to the left. Pull yourself up onto the roof to collect two golden acorns.

Go back down off the roof and continue along the path to reach another wire, which leads up to another pole. Stop short of the pole to attack the next reporter from a safe distance.

You should also watch out for another reporter just below and to the right. Climb down to his level, jump left out of his immediate reach, and quickly send your yoyo to the right to break his camera before he can take a picture.

Climb the ladder down from the pole to reach a roof, head right as far as you can, and then go down to ground level.

On the ground, go all the way left to find Foxy Loxy. Go directly up to her from the "right" side of the dugout and speak to her, ending the level.

# Movie Theater (1)

After his victory at dodgeball, Chicken Little asked Abby to the movies in celebration. Now that his baseball game is done, the pair go to the cinema to watch Commander Ace in action. This level is actually the movie that the pair are watching, rather than Chicken Little's adventures.

You can collect 120 acorns and one golden Ace statue on this level.

## ITEMS

**Coin**

Touching one of these shows the next action you should take, and the controls to perform it.

**Phase gun**

Pick this up to shoot lasers at enemies and other targets.

## DANGERS

Avoid falling into any pools of lava.

Watch out for bursts of lava bubbling out of the pools. Wait for them to pass, or jump over them.

Don't fall through gaps in platforms or other areas into bottomless space!

Shoot the alien walkers from a distance before they can attack.

Keep an eye open for the guns guarding some sections of the hall, and shoot them before they shoot you.

Shoot the red crawlers before they get close enough to sting you with a tail.

Also watch for the green crawlers, which jump down at you from a small height.

Avoid the various attacks of the final boss to finish the level.

# Find the Atomic Acorns!

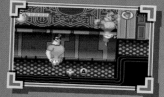

The tutorial coins make a return on this level, showing you how to use some of Ace's special abilities, such as his jump and double jump.

Attack the crumbling stones, using the B button, to break them apart and let you past. Break open even the ones not directly in your path, because they often hold acorns.

To break open the more solid stones, use three quick attacks in a row. These too often hold acorns, so break them apart whether or not they block your path.

Like the slime and water in previous levels, lava pools are dangerous if you fall into them. Jump or double-jump over to the other side.

Break open the four stones clustered together to not only collect acorns and clear your path…

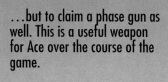

…but to claim a phase gun as well. This is a useful weapon for Ace over the course of the game.

Start watching the lava pools for bursts of lava bubbling up into the air. Either wait for them to die down, or double jump as high as you can to clear them.

With the phase gun in hand, you can shoot stones and other obstacles out of the way, rather than attacking them hand-to-hand.

Once you reach this platform, jump on and then double jump into the air and shoot the red switch to turn it green and raise the platform.

Once the platform reaches its destination, walk right to reach the new hallway and, shortly, the new screen. If you need to return to the lower level, climb on the platform again and shoot the red switch to take it back down.

# Alien Menace

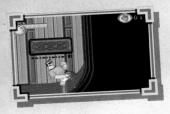

In the second screen, you start to run into strange red sections of the floor and wall. These are special surfaces that Ace can stick to by his feet, even if he's walking straight up a wall or upside-down. Use this surface to walk directly up the wall to the next section of hall.

When you reach a section where the floor drops away out of sight and a silver ball floats back and forth nearby, first drop down the "steps" to the lower level and take that hall.

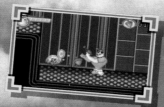  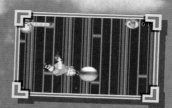 

Before continuing on, make sure you stop at the bottom, turn, and break open the stones to pick up some goodies.

When you reach the end of this bit of hallway, trigger the platform. You can either ride it up and turn back to the left to pick up what you missed, or quickly jump back off the platform, let it rise up alone, and climb back up the way you came.

If you do decide to go back the way you came, when you climb back up to the top, wait for the silver ball to come near and jump over to it. As with the red surfaces, Ace's feet automatically stick to these silver balls, no matter which way he's facing—even upside-down.

In the upper level hallway between the silver ball and the platform, destroy two stones over a pit of lava to collect an acorn and an egg.

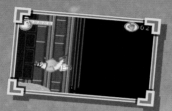   

Back at the platform, jump from it (in its higher position) to the red surface along the wall, and climb.

At the top of the wall, you start to run into the actual alien walkers for the first time. Shoot them from a distance multiple times for the best results. If you get too close, they can attack with their long tentacles.

At the start of the next red surface leading down, make sure you jump up to shoot another stone holding an acorn in midair.

Now climb down the red surface to the lower level, and pick off a gun hanging in midair that's guarding the hall. If you're too slow, it will home in on you and shoot at a distance, so be careful.

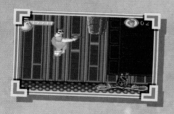  

Climb down one more red surface, ignoring the higher pathway for now, and fight off an alien walker. Then jump into the air to find and destroy another stone.

Just past the second alien walker and near a third, there are two more stones in the air that you might otherwise miss.

**102**

At the end of this lower section, watch out for a red alien crawler, and shoot it before it can sting you with its tail.

Shoot the four stones at the end of the lower hallway to collect a normal, silver, and gold acorn.

Go back to the higher level and this time hop on the silver ball. Make sure you shoot the stones both above and below the ball to collect the goodies.

Although some lava pits have a grill over them to walk across, you still have to watch out for occasional bursts of lava rising up.

# Danger on Every Side

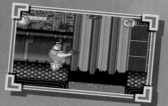

When one red surface ends halfway up a wall, look for another red surface to start on the other side. If that's the case, jump or double jump over to it and continue your way up the wall.

When you reach the top of this wall, look for stones to break ahead and above.

Starting with a lava pit, there are stones over quite a few of the next jumps. In situations like this one, make sure you break the stone before you try to cross, or else you may hit your head when you try to jump the gap and end up falling into the lava instead.

There is a gun in the air just after you step onto the next silver ball. Try to pick it off before you jump on, or be very quick about taking it out as you approach.

The second silver ball moves up and down, so make sure you shoot the stone at the top of its path, and collect the loot.

Jump down to the floor below and watch out for the green crawlers, which jump down at you from a height and attack.

Go to the left and shoot down the gun. Then break open the four stones to collect an egg, and a silver and gold acorn.

Next, go to the right side and shoot down another gun before collecting the items from the rest of the stones—and picking up the golden Ace statue from behind them.

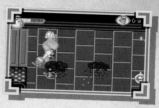

Go back to the floor, orient yourself at the center of the window in the background, and jump upward when the silver ball comes to its lowest point. You latch on upside-down, and you can ride the ball back up into the air.

From the ball moving up and down, jump to another one moving side-to-side to the right when it comes close. Watch out again for more of the guns before you reach more solid land.

When you reach the next pit of lava, note the red surface on the ceiling. Jump up to this, and then walk upside-down along the ceiling back over to safe ground.

Use your unique vantage point to take out a few guns in midair as well, and cross over another gap to solid ground on the other side before jumping down.

# Last Gasp

Fight off the first alien walker, and make sure you don't miss a few stones overhead.

Before you investigate the larger golden spheres in midair, go to the very right side along the ground to break open a few more stones.

When you're done on the ground, check out the large golden spheres. These are much like the smaller silver ones, but when you jump to them, they continue to rotate. You have to either rotate with them or walk around the surface to stay in place.

Jump from one gold ball to the next, but don't miss the stone far overhead.

Jump from the second gold ball to the next hallway, and from there, take another red surface over and down. Before you head to the right a second time, make sure you break open a couple of stones in the lower-left corner. Then jump back up to the red surface and continue on your way.

When you walk along the ceiling over the lava pit, wait for bursts of lava to rise up and then die down before you go through.

Make sure you've collected everything before riding the next platform up. This takes you off the screen and to the last boss fight of the level.

# Tachyon Shields Ready!

The next screen consists of one last boss fight. Once you defeat the boss, you finish the level. This boss hides behind tachyon shields, though, so you have to exploit its openings to take this enemy down.

The enemy has two main attacks that it alternates between. When you see crosshairs like this, move away…

…it means the enemy is about to use a laser in that location, moving it slowly toward Ace's location for a short period of time. If this or another attack hits too often and you lose all of your eggs, don't worry too much. You just start again at the beginning of the boss fight.

The second attack that the enemy uses regularly is a pink ball of energy that moves along the walls constantly until you manage to hit the boss with your own attack. You can tell that this attack is coming when the boss's mouth glows pink.

Between other attacks, the boss may occasionally throw out six spikes from its body. These spikes travel straight out from the center to each of the four corners and also straight right and left. Avoid standing in these spots if possible.

As you avoid the enemy's attacks, you should deal your own as well. Shoot into the open spaces in the boss's shielding. At any given time, there's one side of his shield left open. This changes whenever you land a shot, although you may get in more than one shot at a time if you're quick on the trigger. Be ready to fire into the lower-left, the left side, the upper-left, and then the left side again. After that, the shield openings may change slightly.

After you take down part of the boss's health, it turns violet, and every so often as you take down more health, it grows brighter. Each time the enemy changes color, its attacks get stronger. The laser lasts longer, the pink energy globes are more numerous and move faster, and so on.

After you get the boss's health to zero, you finish the level. One more cutscene runs, showing that Ace's work is not quite done, and you move on to the next chapter.

# Alien Spaceship

Once Chicken Little hits the game-winning run in his baseball game, he calls his friends to his house. It turns out he's been hit in the head yet again, and this time he wants his friends to help before it turns into another "incident." But as Chicken Little is speaking, his friend Fish-Out-of-Water finds the object that hit Chicken Little—and is carried away by it! Now you must take on the role of Fish as he explores the spaceship and tries to find a way out.

You can find 140 acorns and one golden Ace statue on this level.

# DANGERS

Avoid crashing headlong into the stones in your path without breaking them open first.

Don't fall through the bottomless areas beneath some gaps in the flooring.

Wait until the energy barrier lowers, and avoid going through while it's flickering. That means it's about to come back up.

Jump over the balls of energy circling some looped pipes.

# Flying Fish

As you start your playthrough as Fish, note the extra meter on his screen. At the top-center of the screen, you find 0/5 objects listed. This is a record of a strange type of energy source, and how many you've destroyed. To finish the level and move on, you must find and destroy all five of these energy sources.

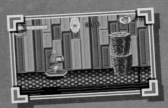

As you slide toward stones in your path, make sure you don't just slam into them unprepared, or you'll take damage. Press B to twirl Fish's platform and break them apart as you hit.

Once you step on one of the pipes going around the room, Fish automatically continues to move quickly in that direction. To get down from the pipe mid-slide, press "Down" and A at the same time. To reach some of the acorns above the pipes, you must jump at just the right time while still moving.

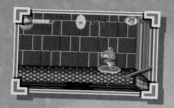

If you don't quite clear the gap and fall to the ground below, head left to climb up the slope, come back out beside the pipe, and then try again.

The second pipe has a gap in the center with a silver acorn over it. To pick up the acorn and clear the hole, jump just as you reach one end of the pipe before the gap.

# Fish Feed

Just inside the second screen, you reach a pit with slick sides and bottom. This works almost like a skateboard ramp. Slide down one side and across the bottom, and use your directional pad to get a little extra "kick" as you go up the next side. Once you reach a level over the rim of the ramp, press A along with a direction to go over the top and onto level ground again.

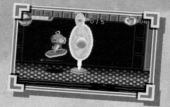

Just past the first ramp, you run into a strange, glowing white object. This is the first of the energy sources that you must destroy. Run into it while pressing B to destroy it with the edge of your platform, and get the first count on your special meter.

Make sure you jump up in time to get the acorn in the gap of the first pipe. Through the gap you can reach the lower level of this screen, or continue along the higher levels. You should visit each level before you go to the next screen, so here we'll take the lower route, through the gap to the floor.

Watch out for these devices scattered around the screen. They form energy barriers at different times, so when they start to flicker, make sure you're not between the two halves of the device. If a barrier is up, wait until it lowers before you cross through, or you'll lose health.

Make sure you pick up one of the rare golden acorns on the lower level, over one of the gaps.

When you dip back down into a ramp, check above both edges of it for an acorn. It requires a high jump after building up speed.

Although you don't want to use them just yet, you can jump on these springs to bounce back up to the higher level.

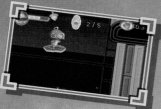

Jump up from the spring after the energy source to find a golden acorn suspended high in the sky.

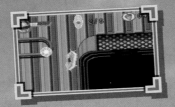

Along the bottom level, you also find the second of the five energy sources you need to destroy.

Once you've finished scouting the bottom half of the screen, go back and start on the top half. From now on, watch for floating balls of energy that circle some of the looped pipes you travel on. If you touch one of these energy balls, you lose a health level. Jump over them if they approach while you're on the pipe.

Game Boy Advance

# High and Low

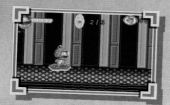

You enter the next screen either high up or down low, depending on which level you exited from on the previous screen.

On the lower level, make sure you get onto a long pipe shortly after the entrance to collect the golden Ace statue.

Now continue along the pipes. When you find one with the next alien energy source over it, jump up partway along the pipe to destroy it. And don't miss the golden acorn below.

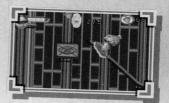

Also make sure to pick up the normal acorn, at a slightly awkward position along the left side of the pipe you used to reach that third energy source.

Now continue to the right, past a couple of the pipes with balls of energy and multiple energy barriers. When you reach two more of the springs, jump on them to reach another of the energy sources, which you can destroy by angling your jump and pressing B as you smash into it. Also note that there's a silver acorn to each side of the energy source, which you can also reach with the two different springs.

# Out of Energy

Once again, you may come into this screen from either a higher or lower exit. Either way, jump over the gap at a three-way pipe intersection and go to the pipe's end. Then turn around and come back to jump onto the pipe you didn't take before, and gather the missed acorn. Then return, take the right-hand pipe, and continue on this time.

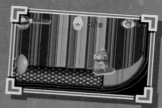

When you reach the springs set on their sides, use them to bounce yourself up the next slope to the top.

When you bounce up like this the first time, make sure you take a left to explore a section you haven't yet seen and collect a few more acorns.

At the end of this section, you slide down another pipe to the left, which in turn leads back down to the original three-way pipe intersection. Now return to where you were, and continue to the right.

Stay on the pipes in the higher section of the screen, and make sure to pick up the acorns during your jumps between the gaps in the various pipes.

After traveling steadily to the right for a while, you reach the final energy source, hanging from the top of the ship. Attack it to break it and finish the level.

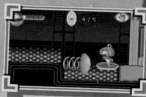

If you miss the energy source the first time through, use the two springs along the floor to bounce back up. Keep trying until you succeed and move on to the next chapter.

# Cornfield

nfield

Thanks to his resourcefulness, Fish has made it outside the spaceship on his own. But now, as the group tries to make their way back through a cornfield away from the ship, the aliens have caught up with them! Direct Chicken Little through the fields and back to the town in time to warn everyone and save the day!

You can find 160 acorns and one golden Ace statue on this level.

## ITEMS

### Coin

Touching one of these shows the next action you should take, and the controls to perform it.

### Ace Coin

Touch this to turn into Commander Ace and use his abilities for a while.

### Soda Machine

Hit this with your yoyo to make it spit out a bottle of soda, which you can use as a rocket.

## Aliens-Attack!

Be especially careful of the falling leaves from trees this time around, because they're even harder to see against the background.

If you've taken any damage, go straight ahead past the trees to collect an egg from this haystack.

Once you've reached the dead end and can't go any farther, go back to find "ledges" among the tree branches that you can climb. Collect the acorns as well.

## DANGERS

Be careful of falling leaves from the trees.

Watch out for falling stalactites in the cave portions.

Don't fall into the water, or you lose an egg.

Avoid stepping into the bottomless holes in the cave.

Avoid the attacks of the UFOs while you knock them out of the sky.

When you reach the end of the "ledges," look right and up to find a strange floating platform. Whenever you see one of these platforms, jump out toward it, and then throw your yoyo out toward that platform (usually) by pressing diagonally in one direction and pressing B. Once the yoyo sticks to the platform, you swing back and forth until you press in one direction at the end of the swing and press A to jump off. Here, pick up the acorns as you're swinging back and forth.

109

Pick up the acorns over the pond here by using the lily pad in your jumps, but be careful that it doesn't disappear on you.

Don't miss the acorn in the air over this long grass, but don't be thrown off by the slower speed of your motions as you try to hit it with your yoyo.

After getting the acorn, fight the UFO just after the long grass. Try to get under the UFO quickly and use your yoyo straight up to strike it. Hit it twice to knock it out of the sky.

Collect the egg from a haystack at the end of the path, if you need it. Then come back and use a head-down jump to break open the boards across a hole leading underground, and climb in.

Watch out for falling stalactites in the cave. When you see them overhead, wait for them to fall, and then go past.

Jump over holes like this, which lead to damage rather than a lower level.

Jump on the mine cart to reach a silver acorn hanging above.

Now you're free to move the cart around as you like. Attack it from the side to move it slightly, or use a Powershot to move it farther. Move it all the way to the right of the cave to reach a ladder, which leads back outside.

At the top of the hole, first turn left. Cross this pond, but watch out for the lily pads, which all disappear at once and then return.

Make sure you go all the way left to the top of the cliff to collect rare acorns. When you're done, head right again and into the next screen.

# Wood and Water

The next series of treetop ledges also includes a bare branch, but don't worry. This acts just like the more leafy platforms.

First, go to the top ledge and collect the silver and golden acorns to the left by swinging from the handy platform.

Go back down to the bare platform, and jump to the right using a series of platforms. Make sure you collect the acorns as you swing along.

This UFO is especially tricky because the grass slows you down quite a bit. You may not have time to get directly under it. If you're good at attacking diagonally, try that to take it down quicker.

x

To cross this pond, you have to time a jump carefully from the edge of the moving log, and then immediately throw your yoyo up diagonally to latch onto the platform and swing from it.

Make sure you pick up the golden acorn, using a swing from a platform, as you make your way through the next series of treetops.

# Buried Treasure

Time your leap from this platform carefully, because the lily pad disappears after a while. When it comes back up, swing to it, and then quickly jump to the next platform and latch on.

Before you climb the next trees, go all the way to the right and head-butt your way down to the next cave.

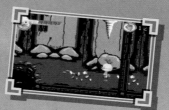

Navigate the next stalactites carefully, because they fall in a pattern of alternating stalactites, all falling at once. Stand beneath one of the alternating ones remaining on the ceiling while the others fall around you.

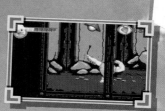

Head all the way to the left to pick up an Ace coin, and bring Commander Ace into the fray for a while.

Game Boy Advance

Break open the stone to the far right, and then pick up the Ace coin to continue as Ace for a short time.

Make sure you pick up the golden acorn, and then destroy the next rock. At this point, you can continue to the next section of the underground caves. But to make sure you don't miss anything, go back out from the caves the way you came, and this time head to the trees.

Climb to the very top of this high series of treetops to collect the acorns, and eventually you reach the top of the high cliff leading farther along your path.

If you've taken damage, step past the hole leading underground to break open this next haystack. It conceals a large egg that heals all of your damage.

Don't go underground just yet. Continue past the haystack to spot a ledge overhead. You can't reach it, and you can't get past the water bordering the tree. But you can jump up and aim a careful diagonal yoyo attack up and to the right. Hit the golden Ace statue hanging over the ledge, and it pick up. Note that you don't really need to do this at this point. There's another way to pick up the statue, later on.

Return to the boards, and break them open to head back underground.

Note that the ladder leading down to the underground area stops short of the ground, so make sure you do everything aboveground before you head down below. You can get back up, but it's tricky.

When you reach the lowest part of the caves, first head left. Jump over this hole carefully to pick up the acorn over it without falling in. Once you reach the spot where you broke open the second stone to cross over to this side, turn around and go to the right side of the caves.

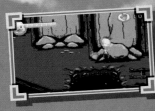

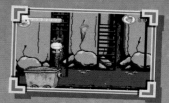

Make sure you use the cart to pick up the acorn hanging in midair between two ladders.

Before using any other ladders, head all the way to the right along the floor to pick up more acorns.

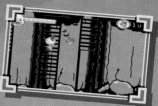

Push the cart far over toward the right, past where you jumped down from above, to reach another ladder within jumping distance from the top of the cart.

First, jump two ladders over to the left to pick up a row of different-colored acorns.

Return to the ladder just above the cart, and this time, make your way to the right along the ladders to climb up and out of the caves.

Go to the right and attack a soda machine with your yoyo. This knocks a bottle of soda out to the right. Walk through it to pick it up, which displays a soda icon in the top-left corner of the screen. When you have a bottle of soda, you can press the right shoulder button to use it as a rocket very briefly. This can shoot you straight up into the air higher than you could ever jump, or shoot you off in another direction.

Go back all the way to the left to find the pond with the golden Ace statue over it, and also two acorns at a slant over the pond. To pick up the acorns and the statue, use the right trigger to activate the soda. As you shake the bottle, press both Up and left to send Chicken Little rocketing up at an angle. If you get the direction and starting point right, you should pick up both acorns on the trip up, and land to pick up the statue at the end of the flight. This is one way to get back to the start of the underground segment. You can also use the bottles of soda to reach the too-high ladders from below.

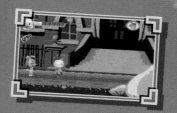

Make your way back to the soda machine, pick up a second bottle of soda, and then continue to the right. Stand just under an acorn you can barely see in the air, and use the right trigger by itself to fly straight up into the air. Pick up two acorns on the trip, and land on a ledge at the end.

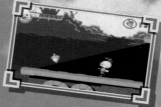

Climb up to the normal roof level, and go to the left to pick up a last silver acorn.

Climb the final ladder up to the bell tower to finish the level.

# Race

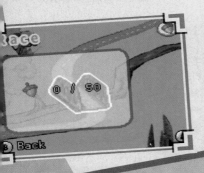

After the bell is rung, at first it looks like this is going to be a repeat of Chicken Little's earlier "incident." But the town soon realizes that this time, the threat is very real. Just as the panic is starting, Chicken Little notices an alien baby wandering around, and realizes that this is the true cause of the alien invasion. Before he can do something about it, though, his father whisks him away from the invasion in the car. Drive the car around the course to make it to the finish line (which also happens to be the starting line) in under two minutes.

You can collect 50 acorns on this course.

## ITEMS

**Tools**

These items repair your car a bit, making it reach its potential more easily. The upgrades help Chicken Little's car.

**Turbo**

Pick up one of these items to restore a bit of energy to your Turbo gauge.

## DANGERS

There are no egg or health meters this time around, but UFOs still cramp your style. Blue and green UFOs are stationary, while reds follow you around for a while.

An oil slick doesn't actually damage your car, but it does make it harder to control for a while. It may even send you off to the sides of the course if you hit one wrong.

## Running in Circles

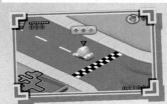

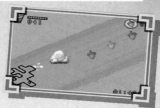

You start the race behind a starting line, which is also the finish line once you make a circuit. You have two minutes on the clock at the bottom-right. To the lower-left is a map of the course, with your position marked. In the upper-left corner is your power gauge, showing how much potential you're getting out of your engine, with your Turbo meter and actual speed just to the right of it.

The acorns for this level are scattered all along the race course, both on the normal track and the shortcuts. If you're missing some acorns, skip some of the shortcuts to collect acorns on the pieces of track along the longer paths.

113

If at any point you get turned around and start to go in the wrong direction, a Wrong Way warning appears on the screen.

Out of all the dangers and pickups, the Turbo restoration is the most important. A successful finish requires taking the shortcuts and having plenty of Turbo to speed your car up for a while.

After you come out of the shortcut and turn left onto the road, watch for the red UFO. It shoots lasers to knock you slightly off course and slow you down a bit, and it also moves along with you for a good distance. This is a good time to use Turbo to shake off its aim and keep moving at a good clip despite the laser fire.

If you don't reach the finish line before the two minutes run out, you lose the race and have to start again. You keep any acorns you've collected, at least.

The first thing to really watch for after setting out is a shortcut along the southeast part of the course. You can barely make out a strip of grass that's darker than the rest. Drive across it to cut a good portion off of your trip. Remember to use a bit of Turbo on straight-aways, even at the start. The first Turbo recharge you pick up isn't as useful if you haven't even used up any of your energy!

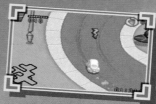

Make sure you take the corner in the right spot to pick up the Turbo recharge, although this can be more difficult with the UFO firing at you. Use Turbo up through this next stretch as well, since the next pickup isn't exceptionally far off.

The second Turbo pickup is between the green and blue UFOs that fire at you from the sidelines.

The next shortcut comes shortly after you turn onto a dirt road. Turn left into the darker green strip of grass…

…and pick up another Turbo charge on the way out of the shortcut. Then turn to the right side of the screen, back onto the track (a left for the car itself).

Just after you come back onto the normal track, another shortcut appears to the south, this time with a set of tools right above it to help you find it easily. Take the shortcut, and this time turn to the left side of the screen when you come out.

Now watch for the next red UFO to appear, with a handy Turbo charge showing up along a large curve shortly after.

The next thing to watch for is a shortcut to the east, at a spot guarded by a blue and green UFO. Make sure you're aimed for the dead center of the shortcut, where you find another Turbo pickup.

When you emerge from the shortcut, watch for another pair of UFOs, and turn north along the normal track this time.

As you approach another curve leading back south, watch for another of the red UFOs trying knock you off course.

Once you reach the end of the curve and start heading west, pick up the next Turbo recharge…

…and watch for yet another one just a bit farther on, on another curve.

As you turn back to the east for the final run to the finish line, weave your way between a whole line of oil slicks alternating north and south along the road.

If you manage to reach the finish line before the clock runs out, you win the race and move on to the next chapter.

# Movie Theater 2

With a lot of action going on in Chicken Little's world, this is a good chance to get away from it all for a while by checking out the last part of the movie. Go back to the theater, select it, and start up the Movie Theater 2 level to see how Commander Ace's quest ends.

You can collect 200 acorns and a golden Ace statue on this level.

*Game Boy Advance*

## ITEMS

**Launcher**

This new weapon adds to your arsenal, giving you a new type of ammunition to use.

## DANGERS

Avoid falling into any pools of lava.

Watch out for bursts of lava bubbling out of the pools, and wait for them to pass or jump over them.

Don't fall through gaps in platforms or other areas into bottomless space!

Shoot the alien walkers from a distance before they can attack.

Keep an eye open for the guns guarding some sections of the hall, and shoot them before they shoot you.

Shoot the red crawlers before they get close enough to sting you with their tail.

Also watch for the green crawlers, which jump down at you from a small height.

Avoid the various attacks of the final boss at the end of the stage.

115

# The Sequel Begins!

Remember to shoot down the overhanging stones before trying to cross the lava, to keep them from interfering with your jumps.

If you need an egg, make sure you destroy this stone, which you might miss if you're not watching carefully for it. It holds an egg to restore your health a bit.

Watch out for the red crawlers off to the sides of the tunnel as you ride the first elevator. Just don't jump off to fight them, or the platform will leave you behind!

Once you find the first golden sphere, make sure you collect the items from stones both to the top right and top left. Make sure you don't let the sphere sweep you under it, where you might be hit by bursts of lava. There's also a stone to the right of the second sphere once you jump to it.

When you reach another lava pit with a stone in front of it, make sure you destroy not only this stone, but the one on the other side of the pit. Then you can jump across safely.

After you reach the large room with a silver sphere, make sure you go right all the way to collect the items from four stones first.

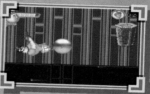

Once you've broken those stones, return to the center of the window in the background and wait for the silver ball to lower. Then jump up to ride it, being careful of the gun that appears to the left, and also destroying the stone to the right.

The second silver sphere is just above the first, and it has a stone to the left and a gun to the right.

After you reach the top of the room, jump up to the red surface along the ceiling. Then head to the left.

First, shoot open four stones and collect the acorns inside…

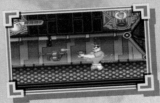

…and then continue past them to collect a new type of gun. You can switch to and from this gun by using the left shoulder button.

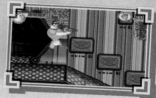

If you need one more egg, don't forget to break open the stone hanging in midair on this side, on your way back to the right to reach the end of the screen.

# Upside-Down and Back and Forth

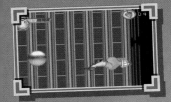

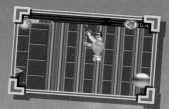

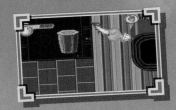

Shortly into the screen, you reach a bit of a tricky passage. Climb up a red surface on a wall, wait for a silver ball to come close enough, and then jump to it.

Learn to judge how far out the sphere moves, and from its farthest point, jump up to another red surface to the upper-left. Don't miss a stone hanging in the air below the red surface.

Most of this section consists of different platforms with red around most of their surfaces. Jump from one platform to another, making your way generally upward and hitting as many platforms as you can. Check the sides and corners of each platform to find one or more stones to break open as well.

When you reach a red surface toward the upper-right of the area, climb down it to break open a group of four stones, which hold two of the rare golden acorns.

When you're done with the stones, return to the red surface, climb up a bit, and wait until a silver sphere approaches. Jump between a series of silver and golden balls, watching overhead for any extra stones to break. Then make your way steadily higher through more platforms, until you reach the end of the section.

# Onward and Upward

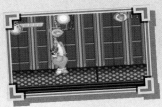

Starting with the first slope, destroy a series of three stones overhead, almost out of sight.

Jump onto a silver sphere, and again jump through a series of silver and golden spheres, this time to the right toward more solid ground. Once again, a whole series of stones hang overhead for you to destroy on your way, and all through the next solid ground, onto the next screen.

Be especially careful of the green alien walkers. When they're defeated, they break apart and two green crawlers emerge from the ruins. So don't stop attacking!

As you move through the fourth section, continue to break apart the stones at varying heights overhead, all along the path.

117

Game Boy Advance

For the rest of the section, you continue to go between silver and golden spheres, alternating with more of the red-surfaced platforms. Keep moving higher toward the exit.

Once you reach a point where you see two side-by-side red surfaces like this, first go right…

…to make sure you break open a set of four stones at the far right. Then return left and take the other route.

After just a little more travel, you reach another golden sphere, this time moving up and down above a red-surfaced platform. Jump to this sphere to ride upward into the final section of the chapter.

# The Final Showdown

After you rise into the final boss's area, you stay on the golden sphere while a cutscene plays. The boss flashes around each of the four corners of the area before the fight begins.

During the fight, the boss randomly teleports to one of the four corners around the sphere. Your job is to move to that location quickly, get off a few shots to damage the boss, and then avoid the return attacks. The boss's health bar is located in the upper-right corner of the screen.

If you're ever knocked from the sphere, you fall onto a green wire that acts as a trampoline. But jump back up quickly! This wire starts to disappear from the two ends very fast, so make sure you get out of harm's way soon.

During the first part of the fight, the boss shoots four missiles per "round" at Commander Ace. Keep firing on the boss as long as you can, and then try to avoid the missiles. If you can hit a missile with a shot, you destroy it before it hits, so shoot all around as you move out of the way.

After the first two sections of the boss's health bar are empty, it changes attacks. Now it uses purple globes of energy that shoot out in streams toward Commander Ace. Shoot at the boss until you see its weapons start to glow violet. Then quickly move around to the opposite side of the golden sphere to keep it between Ace and the bad guy. This blocks the shots.

When the boss has only two sections of health left, his attacks change once again. This time he uses blue waves of energy, but the method of avoiding them is the same—move to the opposite side of the sphere. This time there's no warning, though, so just take a couple of shots and move.

Once you've taken away all of the enemy's health, it self-destructs and you're victorious.

# Town Square

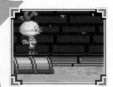

wn Square

After his father took them for a ride around in circles, Chicken Little finally gets the chance to explain what's going on. With the alien baby in hand, they have to make it to the Town Square and get the aliens' attention to put an end to the invasion.

In this level you can find 180 acorns and a golden Ace statue.

## ITEMS

**Coin**

Touching one of these shows the next action you should take, and the controls to perform it.

**Soda Machine**

Hit this with your yo-yo to make it spit out a bottle of soda, which can be used as a rocket.

**Ace Coin**

Touch this to turn into Commander Ace and use his abilities for a time.

*Game Boy Advance*

## DANGERS

Don't fall into the nasty slime and sludge in the sewers.

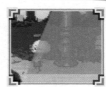

Shoot the alien walkers from a distance before they can attack.

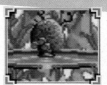

Avoid stepping into the searchlights as much as possible, and if you must walk into one keep moving to avoid being hit with a laser.

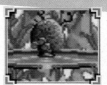

Avoid the attacks of the UFOs while you knock them out of the sky.

## Invasion!

Remember to check the top of each street light for acorns and eggs by using nearby garbage cans or soda machines or other means to get to high ground.

Jump down in the first hole. Move to the left, swinging from the floating platforms.

Pick up a silver acorn from the ground to the left end of the hole before retracing your path to where you first dropped in.

Jump your way across to the right and touch the coin to turn into Commander Ace.

Waste no time in breaking apart two gates to reach a cluster of rare acorns to the far right. Once you've picked them up, head back across to the ladder and climb back up to the soda machine aboveground.

Pick up a bottle of soda from the machine, trigger it with R1, and as you use it press "right" to fly over the large gap.

On the other side go into the searchlight and pick up the acorn from above the bench, but keep moving. Don't stay in the light any longer than you must.

Be careful when you reach the half-crumbled bit of pavement, as this collapses shortly after you land on it. Jump onto it and away to the next bit of sidewalk as quickly as you can.

Use a nearby garbage can to bounce up to this blue awning, and collect the silver acorn on top.

When you reach the next wide gap jump from one jet of water to the next to reach the other side.

At the next soda machine pick up a bottle of pop, then hop down into the sewers nearby. Pick up the large egg to heal all of your damage if you need it.

You can't reach any further underground just now, so climb back up and use the soda to reach the far right side of the large gap. Continue on until you reach this cart. Push it over to a pile of boxes and use it to climb to the top.

Drop into the next sewer and head left across the platforms and floating barrels to collect acorns and reach an Ace coin. Break down the gate between the sewer sections. Now return to your previous point by using the soda bottle to reach the ladder you came down.

This time jump right onto the pipe and use the faucet to turn up the jet of water. Quickly jump on top of the water to ride it up to the higher level—if you miss or fall, stand on the faucet and face left and use "down" + B to turn the faucet back down and try again.

Jump down to the next underground portion and wait for a moving barrel to reach the shore, and jump to it. Jump from this to an unmoving barrel, then to another moving one to cross the pit of slime.

At the top of the next ladder, go left and use the floating platform to cross to a silver acorn.

Jump down into this sewer to pick up a few acorns. Use the faucets to make your way back up to the surface.

You can just barely jump onto this tattered awning from a garbage can. Pull yourself up and pick up the silver and golden acorn from atop the awning.

In the next sewer section, jump from one ladder to the next. Then jump from the higher ladder and latch onto the platform to swing your way across the slime and sludge. Then go up the next ladder to the surface.

When you reach the next vending machine pick up a bottle of soda, jump down to the sewer, and rocket your way across the large gap.

Game Boy Advance

On the other side of the gap pick up the coin to turn into Commander Ace, and double-jump back over the gap you just flew over. Break open the gates to the left of the ladder and pick up the golden Ace statue, then make your way back up the ladder to collect a second soda and use it to fly back across the gap.

Once you've turned back into Commander Ace leap across a series of gaps to the right and break down the large stone blocking the sewer.

Return to the coin and run back across to the right. As Commander Ace, start shooting ahead of you to break down more gates and open the way to the next sewer. There is a silver acorn and large egg you don't want to miss.

Once the gates are down go back to the left, make your way back to the aboveground level.

When you reach the surface, turn left and jump along a series of crumbling platforms to reach a trashcan under a searchlight.

Quickly knock the can over and jump up from it to reach an acorn, then collect the egg to the left of the searchlight if you need the recharge. Continue even further left to pick up a few last acorns.

Go back through the sewers, and this time move past the place where you jumped from one ladder to the next, and instead take the next ladder to the right. From here, climb up to the left.

Climb back up the ladder, and swing along a series of platforms to the right. When you can go no further, jump down to the pavement where you exit to the next screen.

# Grate Expectations

Run forward and use the jets of water as stairs. Be careful not to fall into the slime. At the top of the last jet, jump to the floating platform and use it to swing from.

After making your way past more water jets and another platform, pick up a bottle of soda from the vending machine.

Return to the left and climb down the ladder, then pick up the Ace coin. Use Commander Ace to punch the two large rocks. Pick up the golden acorns in between.

Once you're back to using Chicken Little, jump up onto grates against the wall and climb along them, alternating between grates and floating platforms, to move further right.

Use the soda to boost yourself up to a ladder set higher up in the wall. You may have to fight off an alien walker lurking around the area.

Continue left across crumbling pavement and floating platforms to collect more eggs and acorns.

After you finish with this segment return to the top of the ladder you had started on to travel left, and this time go right, switching between grates and crumbling pavement.

Continue along more crumbling pavement to the second ladder. Climb down to find another coin and use it to turn into Commander Ace.

Travel left and break open a grate separating the sections of sewer. Pick up the large egg only if you really need it...

...as there are a lot of monsters further down the hall.

# Back and Forth

As soon as you enter the next screen you find an egg. Because this egg is so close to the screen it's especially handy—you only need to walk back and forth between the screens to have it reappear. Just watch out for the aliens that also reappear on the other side!

When you're done regaining health, climb the ladder which leads to two more ladders, to the left and right. Take the ladder to the left, and cross back over into the previous section, this time on the top level.

Travel along crumbling pavement and floating platforms all the way left...

...until you collect a group of rare acorns on an edge of the pavement. After you collect the acorns, turn around and cross back over to the next section.

From the top of the ladder, jump to the right-hand ladder. Use barrels and floating platforms to get across safely.

Use the left-hand grate to reach a lamp post that holds a normal and silver acorn.

When you reach the end of this sewer section stand between the two grates and wait for a floating platform to lower close to the ground. Send your yo-yo straight up to latch on to it, and swing back and forth as the platform pulls you up.

To the right, past the grates, travel along one last "staircase" of water to collect the last few acorns.

When you reach the Town Hall, walk in front of it until you trigger a cut-scene. This ends the chapter.

Game Boy Advance

# Alien Mothership

It looks like it's time for the final showdown! Chicken Little has led his group and the baby alien to the alien mothership, where he must now confront the aliens themselves, and explain away this misunderstanding.

There are 220 acorns and a golden Ace statue in this section.

## ITEMS

**Soda Machine**

Hit this with your yo-yo to make it spit out a bottle of soda, which can be used as a rocket.

**Ace Coin**

Touch this to turn into Commander Ace temporarily, and use his skills to get past obstacles.

## DANGERS

Shoot the alien walkers from a distance before they can attack.

Avoid the attacks of the UFOs while you knock them out of the sky.

Watch out for holes that open up in the floor!

Keep an eye out for blue crawlers that tend to lurk in the dark, where they blend in.

Wait until the energy barrier lowers to move through.

Jump over the balls of energy circling some looped pipes.

Avoid the different eye attacks of the final boss of the game!

123

# Darkness Falls

As you begin, the lights dim and Chicken Little is left in the dark, except for a halo of light around him. This continues throughout the level, and the darkness level depends on where he is on the screen.

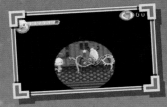

Even in the dark learn to watch carefully for signs of enemy approach. Throw your yo-yo ahead to increase the light around you for a few seconds.

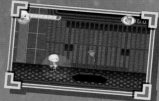

Go right, but watch out! There are panels in the floor that open and close, and if you step on one of these holes while the panel is open, you drop through and lose an egg. Most of them have acorns over them, so that can help you judge where they are.

Once you reach the right-hand wall you find a silver acorn, guarded by a UFO. Collect the acorn and return to the left.

Stop when you reach a lit open area with a window, and wait for a floating platform to descend. Send your yo-yo up to latch on to the platform, and make sure you swing far enough to both sides to pick up two acorns on your way up.

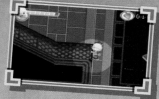

Jump to the left and pull yourself up onto the walkway…

…and continue until you reach a vending machine.

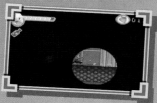

From the start of the slope down, leap up and right to grab onto a ledge and pull yourself up. Travel right along this walkway, jumping over gaps and fighting blue-colored crawlers.

When the light comes back, use your bottle of pop to propel yourself across the longer-than-usual gap, collecting the acorn.

Continue on to the right to pick up a cluster of two acorns and a large egg.

Fall off the next ledge, and at the very bottom make sure you pick up the acorn over the hole, then go right along the walkway. Watch out for more enemies to appear at this stage.

Be especially careful of the UFO over a gap, as it's hard to strike up at it without falling. Try aiming a diagonal attack to take it out quickly.

Watch for the energy barriers that appear, as you make your way further to the right.

Once you reach all the way to the right and jump down to the lower level, pick up a new soda bottle from the vending machine.

Now head left again along this lower level, and watch out for more of the holes that appear. When you reach an Ace coin, you can strike it if you prefer to fight using Ace's longer-range laser for the next few foes.

Claim more acorns and another large egg at the end of the hall.

There is another Ace coin further along, and this time make sure you hit it in order to jump between the three silver spheres to the left.

Use a bottle of soda to fly straight up into the air just to the left of the vending machine.

Grab onto a ledge to the left and pull yourself up. If you miss your mark the first time, get another bottle of soda and try again.

From the small section that's raised higher than the rest of the hall, jump to a moving floating platform. Ride this platform right, and swing from it to get to the next section.

# Into the Light

As soon as you enter the next screen watch out for more blue crawlers.

When you pass a vending machine, make sure you pick up a soda on the way...

...and use it immediately to get past a long gap.

Change into Commander Ace as soon as you see his coin, and use the transformation to walk up the red surface.

Pick up a bottle from the next vending machine...

...and this time use it both "up" and "right" to pick up a diagonal line of acorns.

Continue to the right to reach the exit to the next section.

125

# Multi-Layered

This section is very straightforward. Keep going until you reach a vending machine.

Make sure you pick up a line of acorns on the way, then grab onto the walkway to the right and pull yourself up.

Watch out for floating balls of energy along your path, and jump over them when they come close.

Be careful how you pick up this group of acorns, as you also have to deal with an open panel and a UFO.

You get a chance to recharge with a large egg.

Get another bottle of soda.

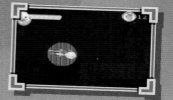

When you're done exploring, use the bottle of soda to fly right over a gap, and into the next screen.

# The Prologue, and the Battle

Go all the way to the right on this screen to get another bottle of pop from this last vending machine.

Line up with an acorn visible from underneath to rocket straight up into the air and collect a column of acorns. Steer to the right to grab onto a walkway and pull yourself up.

Wait for the balls of energy to pass by, then jump so you don't get knocked back down.

The boss fight is against a large alien machine with three eyes. Concentrate on attacking the center eye by jumping and pressing "up" while attacking, as the other two eyes are often elsewhere. The eye can only be attacked when it is not covered by a shield.

When you see one of the lower eyes grow blades around it and start to spin, step away and be ready to dodge. The eye spins fast, then flies away from the alien machine, damaging you as it passes. The eyes bounce high enough that you can run under them if necessary. Watch out for their return trips back to the machine.

Be careful of missiles that launch when an eye is red. You have an advance warning in the form of circles that appear on the ground, and grow as the missile gets closer. Dodge aside before it strikes, then go back to attacking.

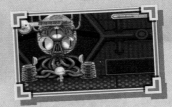

When an eye glows orange, it is charging a laser attack that shoots down at you and moves along the ground. When you see an eye turn this color, step away and wait for a safer time to attack.

Once you take the last bit of health away from the alien menace, all three eyes crack. Enjoy watching Chicken Little save the day, and wait for the credits to roll before continuing on. You can go back to pick up any acorns or other items you missed in the normal levels, or go play more mini-games to rack up even more acorns and buy more improvements.

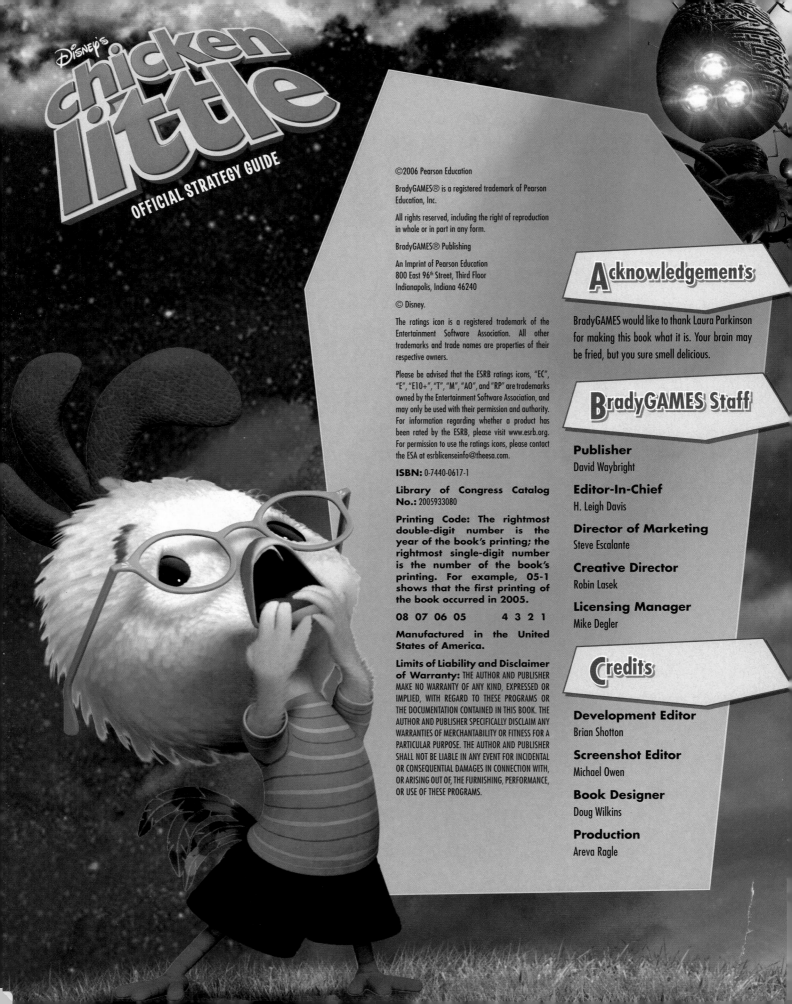

# Disney's chicken little
## OFFICIAL STRATEGY GUIDE

©2006 Pearson Education

BradyGAMES® is a registered trademark of Pearson Education, Inc.

All rights reserved, including the right of reproduction in whole or in part in any form.

BradyGAMES® Publishing

An Imprint of Pearson Education
800 East 96th Street, Third Floor
Indianapolis, Indiana 46240

© Disney.

**ISBN:** 0-7440-0617-1

**Library of Congress Catalog No.:** 2005933080

**Printing Code:** The rightmost double-digit number is the year of the book's printing; the rightmost single-digit number is the number of the book's printing. For example, 05-1 shows that the first printing of the book occurred in 2005.

08 07 06 05          4 3 2 1

Manufactured in the United States of America.

## Acknowledgements

BradyGAMES would like to thank Laura Parkinson for making this book what it is. Your brain may be fried, but you sure smell delicious.

## BradyGAMES Staff

**Publisher**
David Waybright

**Editor-In-Chief**
H. Leigh Davis

**Director of Marketing**
Steve Escalante

**Creative Director**
Robin Lasek

**Licensing Manager**
Mike Degler

## Credits

**Development Editor**
Brian Shotton

**Screenshot Editor**
Michael Owen

**Book Designer**
Doug Wilkins

**Production**
Areva Ragle